Clara Barton

Clara
Barton

Stephen Krensky

DK PUBLISHING

LONDON, NEW YORK, MUNICH,
MELBOURNE, and DELHI

Senior Editor : Shannon Beatty
Editorial Director : Nancy Ellwood
Designer : Mark Johnson Davies
Art Editor : Jessica Park
Production Controller : Charlotte Oliver
Photo Research : Anne Burns Images

First American Edition, 2011

11 12 13 14 15 10 9 8 7 6 5 4 3 2 1
001—180410—June/2011

Published in the United States
by DK Publishing
375 Hudson Street
New York, New York 10014

DK books are available at special discounts
when purchased in bulk for sales
promotions, premiums, fund-raising,
or educational use. For details, contact:

DK Publishing Special Markets
375 Hudson Street
New York, New York 10014
SpecialSales@dk.com

A catalog record for this book is available
from the Library of Congress.

ISBN 978-0-7566-7278-2 (Paperback)
ISBN 978-0-7566-7279-9 (Hardcover)

Printed and bound in China
by South China Printing Co., Ltd.

Discover more at
www.dk.com

Contents

chapter 1

Rustic Beginnings

On Christmas Day 1821, a new baby was about to join the Barton family. Her expectant mother, Sarah, lay in bed under the care of a helpful cousin. Her soon-to-be father, Stephen, sat quietly by the fire in the next room, tired after finishing his daily chores around their farm. The impending event was not a particular worry. His wife had delivered four other children without incident. Captain Barton saw no reason to think this one would arrive any differently. At such times, it was best simply to stay out of the way. Eventually, he was sent off to get the doctor, but the baby girl was born before they returned.

Clara was born in this farmhouse in Oxford, Massachusetts, where her ancestors had settled.

The birth itself was not a surprise, of course. However, the pregnancy had been an unexpected one. Sally, the next youngest child, was already 10, and the oldest, Dolly, was 17. The Barton family

Puritans

The Puritans were a group of English protestants that pulled away from the Church of England in the 1600s and 1700s. Many moved away from England, mostly relocating to the Netherlands and New England.

appeared to be complete. At age 38, Sarah presumably had thought she was done having babies.

As for Christmas, nobody in the Bartons' town of Oxford, Massachusetts, or anywhere else in the young United States, made much of a fuss about it. The Puritans, who had first settled nearby Boston in 1630, had actually banned the holiday from 1659 to 1681. Attitudes had lightened up since then, but many people still treated the day as little different from any other. Two years earlier, in 1819, the famous author Washington Irving had published *The Sketch Book of Geoffrey Crayon*, featuring an English squire who hosted a festive gathering on Christmas. It was a novel idea. But the idea of ordinary families and friends doing the same had yet to catch on.

So the baby remained the center of attention. When the time came, she received the imposing name of Clarissa Harlowe Barton. Clarissa Harlowe was one of her aunts. This aunt had been named for the main character in a book by 18th-century author Samuel Richardson. The Clarissa

in the book was a wealthy young lady manipulated by both her family and her intended husband. She had met a tragic, though fictional, fate. The Bartons could only hope that their little Clarissa's life would turn out better.

Certainly, the country that she was born into had a promising future. In 1821, the United States stretched from Maine in the north to Florida in the south and westward all the way to the Oregon Territory on the Pacific Ocean. The natural resources of that land, most of it still untapped, were vast and varied. The population, now fast approaching 10 million, was expanding rapidly. Of the 24 states in the union, the latest, Missouri, was squarely anchored at the edge of the frontier on the Mississippi River.

Missouri's entry into the United States had not been a smooth one, though. If one issue threatened the country's security,

The signing of the United States Constitution in 1787 had laid the foundation for the new country and its laws.

Unlike farm laborers, slaves were considered the property of their owners with no rights at all.

it was the question of slavery. At the time of the American Revolution, almost 50 years earlier, the former British colonies had allowed slavery within their borders. Four years after winning their independence from Great Britain, the newly liberated states adopted a constitution in 1787 to unite them as a single country. But there was one big catch. While the Northern colonies had little ongoing economic need for slaves, the farming communities of the South relied on the labor-intensive crops of tobacco and cotton. For them, slavery was an integral part of society.

So the Constitution made slavery legal. Doing so might seem to mock the phrase "all men are created equal" from the Declaration of Independence, but the Founding Fathers were willing to overlook that point. They knew that without this concession, many of the Southern states would refuse to join the new United States. Besides, the Constitution had included a provision that banned the importation of slaves as of 1809, and it was hoped the problem would fade away on its own after that.

But the country had no such luck. And by 1820, with free states (those banning slavery) rapidly joining the union,

The Missouri Compromise

The Missouri Compromise of 1820 grew out of the evolving position of slavery in the United States. As of 1808, the importation of slaves was no longer legal, but existing slaves as well as their children could continue to be bought and sold. The Missouri Compromise was an attempt to prevent the regional differences of opinion over slavery from tearing the country apart. It was held in force for a generation, but was never really a satisfactory solution for either side.

the existing slave states got nervous. Soon, they would be hopelessly outnumbered in Congress. At that point they could easily imagine slavery being outlawed. To keep this from happening, they were prepared to vote against allowing any new states at all.

This potential deadlock led to the Missouri Compromise of 1820. It laid out a future in which slavery in the western territories would not be allowed. But more immediately, it established that free and slave states would enter the union in pairs. Both pro- and antislavery political factions hoped that the issue would now subside, though not everyone was so optimistic. Some, like 77-year-old Thomas Jefferson, feared that the Compromise would someday tear the country apart.

For the moment at least, such large issues had little effect on daily life in Oxford. The small farming and milling community lay 50 miles west of Boston on the way to Connecticut. It had been founded in 1713, and Samuel, the first Barton to settle there, had arrived only three years later.

His grandson Stephen had been a doctor and fought in the Revolutionary War. It was his son, also named Stephen, who had married 21-year-old Sarah Stone in 1804 and eventually became the father of Clarissa.

Clara's parents were prominent citizens in the town. Captain Stephen Barton, as he was known (though he had served in the army as a common soldier) was decidedly old-fashioned. He didn't enjoy wasteful activities like dancing or drinking. As a young man in the 1790s, he had served in the army on the western frontier in Ohio and Michigan. And he always retained his military bearing. He was skilled with his hands and had built his own house, as well as much of the furniture inside it. He farmed his own land, raised horses and took part in local politics. The captain believed in hard work, but he was also charitable toward the poor. One of the founders of the local Universalist Church, he supported education and religious tolerance. His youngest daughter later recalled him as a calm and reasonable man.

The same could not be said of Clarissa's mother. Sarah Barton also came from a military background. Her

The Revolutionary War was a living memory during Clara's childhood, since many older men had served in it.

Clara's parents, Stephen and Sarah Barton, were serious people who worked hard and prospered.

father, David Stone, had been a sergeant during the revolution. Sarah would have made a tough soldier herself, with her strong temper and stubborn ways. She too had little time for idle hands. She rose early to oversee her household, a place she ruled with an iron fist. She was thrifty to a fault, often feeding her family old fruits and vegetables that were just barely edible—and woe to anyone, even her husband, who crossed her. Once Stephen bought a new iron stove without consulting her on the purchase beforehand. Sarah was not pleased. She took the stove apart piece by piece. Then she threw it into the nearest pond.

In this household, the littlest Barton started to grow. Though formally named Clarissa, her name was too much of a mouthful for daily use. Various nicknames came and went, but Clara was the one that stuck. Little Clara was eager to learn, and her older sisters and brothers were happy to help. Dolly taught her to read at three, and Stephen and Sally covered other academic subjects.

Her brother David was very firm about the particular things she should know how to do. One was throwing a ball like a boy. Two was being familiar with the use of basic tools such as hammers and screwdrivers. And three was knowing how to tie knots that would not come undone.

In other ways, though, Clara led a typical life on a farm. There were chores to do, like milking the cows or picking vegetables from the fields. She fed chickens and gathered eggs. Clara's earliest memory—she couldn't have been more

Horses were a staple of 19th-century farm life, useful for plowing fields and for transportation.

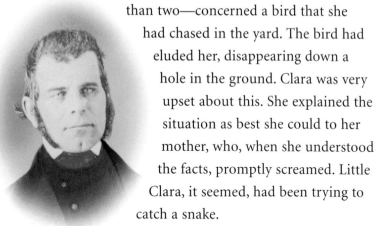

than two—concerned a bird that she had chased in the yard. The bird had eluded her, disappearing down a hole in the ground. Clara was very upset about this. She explained the situation as best she could to her mother, who, when she understood the facts, promptly screamed. Little Clara, it seemed, had been trying to catch a snake.

Clara's brother David spent his life working in Oxford, in the family milling business and on the family farm.

Catching a snake might have seemed like fun to Clara because her mother believed that children in general didn't need toys, and that girls in particular didn't need dolls. They did, however, need to learn cooking, sewing, and other domestic skills. And Sarah made sure Clara took these lessons to heart.

Clara's father, meanwhile, gave her a chance to exercise her imagination. "I listened breathlessly to his war stories," she later recalled. "Illustrations were called for, and we made battles and fought them. Every shade of military etiquette was regarded. Generals, colonels, captains, and sergeants were given their proper place and rank." Much to Stephen's delight, Clara loved sharing in his memories. And she could keep track of the players and what they were supposed to do.

Her most constant companion, however, was a white-haired dog named Button. She appreciated Button's company because she was rather shy. "I had no playmates," she wrote many years later, "but in effect six mothers and fathers. All took charge of me, all educated me, each according to personal taste. My two sisters were scholars and athletic, and strove in that direction. My two brothers were strong, ruddy, daring young men, full of life and business."

Although Clara never pursued life as a farmer, her fondness for horses remained strong throughout her life.

Even though Clara was much younger than her brother David, she spent a considerable amount of time with him. David was passionate about horses, and shared his interest with his little sister. He loved to take her along with him into a field. There, he would grab the reins of two barely tamed colts, throw Clara on the back of one and himself on the back of the other. Clara was fearless in her determination to keep up. David told her to "cling fast to the mane," and they would "gallop away over field and fen, in and out among the other colts in wild glee . . ."

It was a precious time of freedom in her life that she thoroughly enjoyed.

"I had no playmates, but in effect six mothers and fathers."

—Clara Barton, in her memoirs

chapter 2
Growth Spurts

"**I** was what is known as a bashful child," Clara confessed in later years. This was not surprising considering that she was surrounded by her family and had little contact with strangers. But shyness was not considered a virtue. In the hope of correcting this deficiency, her parents decided to send her to a nearby boarding school. It was quite a change. At home, she had been the only student, learning from her brothers and sisters. Now there were 150 students filling several schoolrooms. And almost all of them were bigger and older than she was.

The idea that all children should go to school to gain an education only gradually took hold in 19th-century America.

Life on the farm was both hard in its daily obligations, and unpredictable in its dependence on good weather.

Clara was good at her studies, but speaking up with dozens of eyes staring at her was unnerving. She grew pale and lost weight. At the end of her first term, her parents, her teachers, and her family doctor held a meeting. They decided it would be best for Clara to return home.

But home had changed. Her family was moving down the hill to a 300-acre farm. The new house needed to be fixed, and Clara pitched in to help. Among other things, she learned how to hang wallpaper and make her own paints.

Some cousins came to live with the Bartons as well. Clara's big sisters had stayed at the old house, which made the change feel even more dramatic. On the bright side, Clara's cousins were closer to her own age. "From never having had any playmates, I now found myself one of a very lively body of six—three boys and three girls . . ."

Clara and her cousins explored the new farm thoroughly, learning the best spot to cross the streams and where to find the tastiest chestnuts. They played hide-and-seek and balanced on poles in the millstream. Clara's parents, worried that she was becoming too much of a tomboy, forbade her from learning

Clara always liked a challenge. As a young girl, she learned how to ice skate in secret, since her parents disapproved.

to ice skate. But it was a little late to rein Clara in now. She enlisted the boys to teach her secretly at night. They pulled her along, one on each side, which was fine, as long as the ice was smooth. But, as Clara remembered, "at length we reached a spot where the ice had been cracked and was full of sharp edges." Here, she fell repeatedly, injuring herself seriously enough that her parents soon found out. They were not pleased, and Clara endured several weeks of their disappointment before life went on as before.

In warmer weather, she continued to practice riding— now with her own horse. Riding became second nature to her, and she remembered the skill well later in life. But not every advance was planned or predictable. In 1832, when she was 11, her brother David was helping to build a new family barn. He was working on the ridgepole when a plank snapped beneath him and he fell to the ground. At first he seemed to be largely unharmed by the accident, but his internal injuries turned out to be serious.

RIDGEPOLE

A ridgepole is the horizontal beam that runs along the peak of a roof. The upper ends of the rafters are attached to it.

Rural communities often came together for barn raisings, group efforts to build a barn.

No one had to tell Clara what she should do next, and she didn't need to ask. She simply knew it in herself. She took care of David day and night, rarely leaving his side. And he grew just as attached to her in return. Clara learned to administer his medicine and manage his treatment with great aplomb. Among her many duties was applying the leeches that were supposed to suck the bad blood out of David's body.

For two years, Clara tended to her brother, leaving him for only half a day in all that time. He recovered at last, no thanks to the leeches, due to rest and the ability of his body to heal over time.

Clara's devotion was not unheard of in the

The Practice of Leeching

For thousands of years, leeching was a favored medical practice for removing "bad" blood from a sick person. This was accomplished by attaching leeches, a kind of wormlike creature with suckers at both ends, to the patient's body. The procedure often made the patient weak enough to die from other causes. However, it was an accepted medical practice until the late 1800s.

In many rural communities, where doctors were scarce, midwives provided various medical services.

Barton family. Her great aunt Martha Ballard, who died a few years before Clara's birth, had been a well-respected midwife. She had delivered babies and treated illnesses across a wide swath of the wilderness of Maine. Caring for her brother had given Clara a special satisfaction. It was something she would always remember.

As delighted as Clara was to see David recover, she had trouble simply returning to a life of her own. The freedom to do as she pleased was no substitute for the feeling of usefulness she had felt nursing her brother back to health. She felt anxious and unsettled and cast about for some meaningful way to fill her time.

For the moment, she stayed busy doing chores around the farm and helping to look after her sister Sally's children. As time passed, though, she roamed farther from home, coming to the aid of poor families in the nearby countryside. Some had illnesses that she tended to. Others had money troubles, and she tried to point these families in a direction where they could get assistance.

None of this activity, however, was helping Clara decide how to spend her life. And at the ripe old age of 15, Clara's lack of focus troubled her mother. Sarah shared her frustration with a visitor, L.N. Fowler, who was staying with the family for a few weeks while lecturing in the area.

Mr. Fowler was a phrenologist, a respected scientific occupation at the time. According to phrenology, various skills and personality traits were housed and controlled in different places of the brain. A person's development in these areas was revealed through bumps in the skull. A skilled phrenologist could feel and interpret the meaning of these bumps with his hands.

During the early 19th century, the population of the United States was centered on its agricultural communities.

The science of phrenology has been disproved, but it was widely used in Clara's day to predict character traits.

Although there was no scientific truth to this pursuit, many phrenologists were quite sincere in their attempts to gain insights into human nature. Fowler made a study of Clara, observing both her shyness and her helpful personality. Unlike many young women of her time, he noted that she desired to work, to have an occupation outside the home.

For Fowler, Clara's path was clear. She should become a teacher, one of the few jobs open to women, and one in which he thought she would thrive. This pronouncement was unwelcome to the shy girl standing before him. Clara could imagine few situations worse than the one he described. Why would she be willing to speak alone in front of a room full of young strangers? It seemed a horrible fate. And yet what were her realistic alternatives? There were few professional opportunities at the time for women seeking to work. Perhaps it was pointed out to her that the young students would no longer be strangers once she had spent some time

with them. The awkward period of introduction would pass soon enough. And what about the opportunity to influence young minds, to get the students started toward useful lives of their own? Surely there would be great satisfaction in that.

It was something to think about. As the months passed, Clara's opposition to the idea softened. She went for an interview, an examination with the local school board. "How well I remember the preparations . . . the efforts to look larger and older, the examination by the learned committee of one clergyman, one lawyer and one justice of the peace . . ."

Whatever her reservations, she passed the inspection with the school board. And when the next spring came, she decided to give teaching a try.

In an era when many could not read or write, teachers were not required to get advanced degrees to teach.

chapter **3**

Learning and Teaching

On a bright May morning in 1839, Clara Barton approached District School Number 9 in North Oxford, Massachusetts. This was the place where she was to begin her teaching career. The school was neither large nor new, and no more distinctive than its name. Still, Clara was determined to make the best of it.

"On entering, I found my little school of 40 pupils all seated according to their own selection, quietly waiting with folded hands. Bright, rosy-cheeked boys and girls from four

to thirteen, with the exception of four lads, as tall and nearly as old as myself. These four boys naturally looked a little curiously at me, as if forming an opinion of how best to dispose of me . . ."

Clara may not have originally sought out a career as a teacher, but she took the position very seriously.

Early schoolhouses, like this one in Massachusetts, were simple buildings with very basic facilities.

Clara hoped to make a positive connection with her students. However, her first chance to do so did not come in the classroom. It presented itself outside on the playground. There, she joined in some of the students' games. Even the oldest, most troublesome boys had to admit that she was good at them. This skill dramatically improved their opinion of her. Maybe this new teacher would be worth listening to after all.

It was a challenge to maintain order and interest across such a wide age range, but Clara managed it masterfully. A few students may have had the ambition to continue their educations beyond high school. The rest only wished to learn what they needed to get on with their lives—how to read, write, and compute simple sums—and to memorize some geographical facts.

Clara soon gained a reputation, both within the school district and in nearby towns, for preserving discipline. This was a distinct accomplishment. However, it did not dispel the doubts she felt about her background. She was always questioning whether she had really received enough education herself to be educating others. Her parents had no reservations, though. They were pleased to see her professionally settled. So when an opening in the nearby town of Charlton opened up, they strongly encouraged her to take it.

A little reluctantly, Clara accepted the position. She quickly found that there were two big differences between her old job and her new one: One was that Charlton was too far away for her to continue living at home. The other was that the unruly boys in her new class were less willing to behave themselves. Clara tried to reason with them. When that failed, she talked with their parents.

Whipping students was a common form of punishment in schools during Clara's time as a teacher.

But nothing seemed to help.

Finally, her patience ran out. One morning, the boys' ringleader arrived late and immediately began disrupting the lesson. Clara called him to the front of the class. When he lazily approached, she pulled out a riding whip—and used it. Harsh discipline was common enough at the time, but the whipping left both the boy and

Clara shaken. After that, he stopped causing trouble in her classroom. And in the future, she never resorted to such a drastic step again.

> *"I may sometimes be willing to teach for nothing, but if paid at all, I will never do a man's work for less than a man's pay."*
>
> —Clara Barton, in her memoirs

Clara always took her teaching seriously. Some women taught only to fill the time before they were married, but Clara, despite her original hesitations, treated teaching like a career. In some ways she felt that her students were receiving the education that she had never gotten herself.

Her first salary was two dollars a week, the usual sum for women teaching the less-important summer terms. Then the town of Oxford offered her a position teaching the winter term in a difficult school. It was a compliment to her reputation since this was considered a man's job. However, the proposed pay was no different than what she was already earning. Clara objected. "I may sometimes be willing to teach for nothing," she explained to the board, "but if paid at all, I will never do a man's work for less than a man's pay." After due deliberation, the school board changed their offer and met her demand.

As dedicated as Clara was to teaching, not all of her time was spent on work. There were outings with friends, and perhaps a romance or two that never quite stuck. One

highlight from this time was her brother David's wedding, in which

Clara's first view of the Atlantic Ocean, during a visit to Maine, made a big impression on her.

she served as a bridesmaid. The marriage took place in Maine. Oxford was only 50 miles from the seashore, but it was on this trip that Clara first saw the Atlantic Ocean.

After returning home from the wedding, she helped reorganize the Oxford school system. Her brother Stephen was both a mill owner and a member of the school board. The success of the Barton mill and others like it had led to a bump in the local population. However, there was no school in the area where the mill workers lived, which meant that they and their families were denied the chance to get an education. And some townspeople questioned whether they were obliged to support the lower classes with a school.

This attitude infuriated Clara. Poor and underprivileged children deserved respect and consideration as much as anyone else. There were no two ways about it. Clara worked with Stephen to get a new school built in town. She also helped design the new school, shaping it from the beginning as a place of learning and not just as another building that happened to be a school, but could just as easily have been something else.

Naturally, Clara became the school's first teacher. Many of her students, who ranged in age up to their early twenties, were immigrants whose English was far from perfect. Among other things, Clara introduced the idea of having the students read aloud to improve their language skills.

Despite these successes, Clara felt hemmed in professionally. She was proud of her teaching accomplishments, but given her own limited education, she could only achieve so much. Nine years had passed since she had started teaching. When she looked back, she saw time "in which I should have been in school myself, using time and opportunities for my own advancement which could not be replaced. This thought grew irresistibly upon me, until I decided that I must withdraw and find a school, the object of which should be to teach me something . . ."

The Barton family mill, like others of the period, used water power to run their machinery.

After investigating her options, Clara applied to—and was accepted at—the Clinton Liberal Institute, a coeducational academy in Clinton, New York. This meant uprooting herself and moving almost 200 miles away—a decision she did not take lightly.

Clara arrived on a cold January day in 1850. She was not sure how she would react to the classes, but once they began, she was very pleased with the experience. One of her teachers, Louise Barker, was truly inspirational. She had a kindly and inviting manner that Clara found exhilarating.

Throughout her life Clara would make use of the studious habits she developed while pursuing her education.

The subjects Clara studied included advanced mathematics, foreign languages, history, philosophy, and the natural sciences. Clara was at least a few years older than most of her fellow students, and she kept her teaching background a secret so as not to draw undue attention to herself. She actually enjoyed her time in Clinton so much that she didn't even return home during vacations.

Finally, after successfully completing her three terms of school, she returned to Oxford in the summer of 1851. In some ways, the town seemed the same. But sadly, there was one significant change: Her mother had died while she had been away, and that was a hole in her life not easily filled. Her father was now over 70 and living with her brother, David. The 29-year-old Clara could muster no enthusiasm for settling back into the rut of her old life, but this fact didn't mean she knew what to do next.

Into this void came an invitation from Charles and Mary Norton, two of her friends from Clinton who lived in Hightstown, New Jersey. The Nortons were much younger than Clara (21 and 16, respectively) but they had all gotten along well during their studies. In times past Clara might have declined their offer, wary of leaping into the unknown. Now she jumped at the chance.

The Nortons were gracious hosts, and their family was prominent in the town's affairs. When a nearby teaching opportunity opened up, Charles and Mary's father asked Clara if she would be interested in the job. Clara had continued to keep her earlier teaching experience a secret, so she agreed to take the position only if Mary could come with her to help out.

Clara's new classroom in New Jersey was much like the ones she had left behind in Massachusetts. The

The McGuffey Readers were a staple of American education during the 19th century.

This school opened by Clara Barton in Bordentown, New Jersey was later named for her.

students were similar too, their attitudes ranging from wide-eyed curiosity to sullen resentment. Some of the boys had a reputation for being disruptive, but Clara disarmed them by calling on the ringleader and asking him to help her break all the switches that their old teacher had used to whip them. Of course, she explained that, without the switches, she would now need his help to keep order and set a good example.

Clara also made a point not to simply lecture the students for hours on end. She walked among them, breaking down barriers of formality and making the classroom a more comfortable place. As before, she joined in their games at recess. Only one aspect of the situation was troubling. While public education was free in Massachusetts, New Jersey families has to pay for their children's education. This meant that poor children could not afford to be educated at all.

Clara wanted to change that. She went before the local school board with a petition to start a new school in New Jersey. Her only wish was that it must be a school where any child could go freely. And to underscore the point, she declared that she would not need a salary.

Under such favorable terms, the board agreed to her request, and opened a school in Bordentown. Only six boys showed up on the new school's first day, but their numbers soon grew. Within a year, Clara had hundreds of students and had hired other teachers. Bordentown had even built a new school to house the students, a testament to Clara's success.

There was just one problem: In 1853, the idea of a woman being in charge of a sizable institution was unthinkable. So a male principal was hired to administer the new school. If he had been a capable and congenial colleague, Clara might have made the best of it. But the new principal was jealous of her local stature. He made her working day so unpleasant that her health suffered. She became nervous and jittery, and she eventually lost her voice. Reluctantly, she realized that her new school was going to have to get by without her.

Horace Mann

Horace Mann (1796–1859) was an American politician and educator. As the secretary of the newly created Massachusetts Board of Education in the late 1830s, he advocated free public education as the best way to turn children into productive citizens. He also believed in better-trained teachers. The pattern he established in Massachusetts influenced Clara's work in the New Jersey school system.

chapter 4

Ups and Downs

Still upset about her disappointment in New Jersey, Clara decided to move further south. She hoped the milder winters in Washington, D.C., would help improve her health, especially her voice, which remained fragile after her experience in Bordentown.

In 1854, the nation's capital was not a booming metropolis. It was a sleepy city of just a few thousand people. Its accents and customs were Southern as were most of its inhabitants. Washington was a municipal island, independent of neighboring Virginia and Maryland. Its 61 square miles were directly administered by the United States Congress.

The United States Capitol underwent several renovations as Washington grew up around it.

The architect Pierre Charles L'Enfant had grandly laid out the city in 1791 at President George Washington's request. As L'Enfant envisioned it, the grid of streets would radiate outward from the future United States Capitol. But 60 years later, much of his plan still existed only on paper. The swampy landscape was particularly unpleasant during the hot and humid summer months, so almost everyone left town until cooler temperatures returned

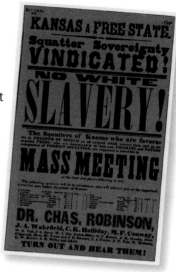

The Compromise of 1850 provoked a strong response from the public, which led to meetings across the country.

in the fall. The occasional handsome government buildings were outnumbered by ramshackle wooden structures, and there were only a few sidewalks. The Capitol itself was undergoing a considerable expansion when Clara arrived, most notably receiving an iron dome to replace the smaller copper-and-wood one that no longer seemed to fit.

Changes in architecture, however, were the least of the challenges Washington was facing. The issue of slavery still hung heavily over the nation's fortunes. In 1848, following the Mexican War, California and significant parts of the Southwest had been added to the union. The Compromise of 1850 had settled for the moment where slavery would be allowed in the new Territories, but neither the pro- nor

Alexander DeWitt (1798–1879) served in Congress before returning to his job in the textile industry.

the antislavery sides were entirely happy with the results. Tempers flared again over the Kansas-Nebraska Act of 1854, which repealed the Missouri Compromise of 1820, and allowed the possibility of slavery in previously free territories. One critic of the new bill was a tall, gangly lawyer from Illinois, a largely unknown former congressman named Abraham Lincoln.

In Washington, Clara soon met a politician from her home district in Massachusetts, Alexander DeWitt. Sympathetic to her situation as a newcomer to the city, he invited her to several social functions. Among those she met through his connections was Charles Mason, who was the commissioner in charge of the United States Patent Office. Mason had the power to hire temporary clerks, and he was committed to streamlining the patent process so that more inventors would register their ideas.

Mason liked Clara, and hired her to work for him. She had mastered a formal style of handwriting that mimicked engraved printing, and she put it to good use. Her days were spent copying patents, rules and regulations, and other documents that needed to be in more than one place at a time. At first, she had only good things to say about her appointment: "My situation is delightfully pleasant. There is . . . not a single disagreeable thing to do, and no one to complain of me."

In those days, the Patent Office did more than just evaluate and process inventions. It served much like a museum, sending out expeditions to collect artifacts and specimens, particularly those with a North American connection. Of course, inventions themselves remained the focus. The pitchfork had been patented in 1850, having been barely preceded by the safety pin. The first sewing machine came in 1855. A newly designed handgun, a revolver from partners Horace Smith and Daniel Wesson, appeared the following year.

In time, Clara's evident intelligence gained her a promotion. She was put in charge of sensitive material that had to be kept

The United States Patent Office was the destination of any inventors who wished to register their work.

confidential. The person who previously held the position had not been good at keeping secrets. Clara was. She was also proud of her salary of $1,400 a year—equal to what a man would be paid.

Unfortunately, Commissioner Mason left the patent office in 1855 to return home to Iowa. His successor was eager to curry favor with the old-fashioned secretary of the interior, Robert McClelland, who disapproved of having women in the workplace. This was due to what he called the "obvious impropriety in the mixing of the two sexes within the walls of a public office." Clara, along with four other female clerks, was removed from her position solely so that a man could have her job instead.

Clara was demoted to being a copyist, a job in which she received no salary, but was paid meagerly by the piece for the work she produced. As she described it in a letter to her sister-in-law Julia, she spent three months wading through "3,500 pages of dry lawyer writing." She copied parts off of every page until she had compiled "a great volume almost as heavy as I can lift."

> *"He did not approve of having women in the workplace due to what he called the 'obvious impropriety in the mixing of the two sexes within the walls of a public office.'"*
>
> —Clara Barton on Robert McClelland

It didn't help matters that the office was no longer a pleasant environment. The men there were not pleased to have a woman working among them. They made jokes at her expense and insulted her. They blew smoke in her face and spit tobacco juice at her feet. In their eyes, Clara was filling a job that could have gone to a man. It was outrageous. They felt that a man would obviously be more deserving of the position—regardless of the skills Clara possessed.

Robert McClelland (1807–1880) was the governor of Michigan before becoming secretary of the interior.

Her situation improved somewhat when Commissioner Mason returned to Washington. However, he was not able to simply install Clara in her old job. In any event, the election of 1856 brought James Buchanan, a new president, into the White House. It was common practice for some government employees to lose their jobs when a new presidential administration began, and this time was no different. In addition, after Buchanan was elected, those with antislavery views were considered vulnerable, and Clara had not been shy about expressing her opinion on the subject. She had been deeply moved by Senator Charles Sumner's speech "The Crime Against Kansas," which he had read in the Senate in May 1856. A famous orator, Sumner had railed against the Kansas-

Nebraska Act, which widened the areas in which slavery would
be allowed. He also made personal attacks on the two primary
backers of the bill, fellow senators Stephen A. Douglas of Illinois
and Andrew Butler of South Carolina. "It was an oration of
greater power than any I ever knew. It was upon this very point
of the extension of slavery, and it settled it . . . I have often said
that that night war began!" Not everyone had an easy time
choosing sides in the debate, though. Many people who were
staunchly opposed to slavery still hesitated to advocate their
position knowing it could tear the country apart.

James Buchanan (1791–
1868) is most famous for
being the only bachelor
ever elected president of
the United States.

By the summer of 1857,
Commissioner Mason was gone again,
and in September Clara was told that
her services were no longer needed.
Fortunately, she now had enough savings
to live where she pleased, and staying
in Washington had, for the moment,
lost its appeal. She headed north,
ending up back in her home town.
It was good to see her relatives
again. She stayed with her brother
David and his family, at their house
in Oxford. Offers came in for her
to teach in local schools, but she
turned them down. Clara didn't
know what she would do next,
but she wasn't ready to commit to

staying in one place. Eventually, she moved a few miles east, where she took classes to further her education. If she chose to become a governess or teach

GOVERNESS

A governess is a woman hired to care for and educate children in the home.

in a private academy, at least she would be prepared.

As it happened, her plans were derailed by various family members, who came to her for emotional and financial support. She contributed both, which proved to be a serious drain on all her resources. Seeking a change of scene, she went to New York City. Her aim was to find a job, but her health was not up to the attempt. Unable to recover on her own, she went to see some friends of hers, who gave her a warmer welcome than her family had done.

Clara still intended to go back to New York. It seemed the most promising place for her to work. But then she received an unexpected note: A new president, Abraham Lincoln, was moving to the White House, and the government was turning over its jobs once again. If she wanted, Clara could return to the Patent Office. She would be copying documents for low pay, but at least the job was familiar—and she did miss her friends in Washington.

Clara accepted the offer.

The Kansas-Nebraska Act provoked strong reactions in the western territories of the country.

chapter 5
Angel of the Battlefield

The Washington, D.C., that Clara Barton returned to in 1860 was a very tense place. Many years of attempted reconciliation over the issue of slavery had frayed the patience of the whole country. Nerves were fast approaching a breaking point—and nowhere was this felt more strongly than in the nation's capital. Three years earlier, the Supreme Court had handed down a decision in the case of the black fugitive Dred Scott, who was trying to win his freedom from his master because they had spent some time living in a free state. The Court did not look kindly on his petition. Among other points discussed, the Court stated that blacks were "beings of an inferior order, and altogether unfit to associate with the white race, either in social or political relations, and so far inferior that they had no rights which the white man was bound to respect." That was bad enough, as far as the

Dred Scott (1799–1858) was famous for taking his case before the United States Supreme Court.

antislavery forces were concerned. But the Court wasn't done. It added that the Missouri Compromise of 1820 was unconstitutional, and that Congress had no power to limit the spread of slavery along geographic lines.

The secession movement, depicted here, gained momentum once Abraham Lincoln was elected president.

Essentially, the Court was legally returning the nation's slavery policy to the time of the Founding Fathers. Still, the tide against slavery was rising because a growing majority of the national population was against it. Down South, sentiments bristled at such talk. As pressures on both sides mounted, talk of secession filled the air. The Southern states would sooner break the country apart than give up one of their most cherished rights. Extinguishing slavery was not an

SECESSION

Secession is the act of withdrawing from membership in a larger group.

Confederate soldiers, like this boy, came from every section of Southern society, and some of them were very young.

acceptable option in the states where it had flourished.

The incoming president, Abraham Lincoln, was so hated in the South that, aside from Virginia, his name had not even appeared on the ballots in the Southern states. The reason for this intense dislike was attributable to Lincoln's statements on slavery. In a famous 1858 speech, he had declared that where slavery was concerned, he wished to "arrest the further spread of it, and place it where the public mind shall rest in the belief that it is in the course of ultimate extinction."

So it was not truly surprising when the Union began to unravel. In late December 1860, more than two months before Lincoln's scheduled inauguration, South Carolina declared itself to be no longer part of the United States. Over the next few weeks, six other states—Georgia, Florida, Mississippi, Alabama, Louisiana, and Texas—did the same. On February 4, 1861, they formed the Confederate States of America. The Confederates installed Jefferson Davis as their new president and declared their intent to go forward as an independent nation.

Clara did not see how any secession movement could be permanent. She believed it "to be wearing out in its infancy and if wisely left alone will die a natural death, long before maturity." Nonetheless, she was troubled by the increased boasts of Southern supporters she heard around Washington. "Nothing is or has been more common than to see little spruce clerks and even boys strutting about the streets and asserting that 'we had no government—it merely amounted to a compact but had no strength.'"

The United States, under its Constitution did not recognize the right of any state, North or South, to remove itself from the union. So in his inaugural address in March 1861, President Lincoln tried to reassure the nation that the differences among the states were not as dire as many people clearly believed. There was no reason for Southerners to feel threatened by the inauguration of an antislavery president, he insisted. "I have no purpose, directly or indirectly, to interfere with the institution of slavery

Jefferson Davis (1808–1889) was a senator from Mississippi before becoming president of the Confederacy.

in the States where it exists. I believe I have no lawful right to do so, and I have no inclination to do so."

Fort Sumter was built after the War of 1812 as one of a series of fortifications along the southern Atlantic coast.

Clara Barton heard these words for herself because she attended the ceremony. She hoped the Southern states would accept Lincoln's speech in good faith and retreat from the warlike stance they had assumed. But events had passed the point where words alone could pull them back. In April, Lincoln ordered the blockade of Southern ports. This act could not go unchallenged. On April 12, Southern forces in Charleston, South Carolina, began firing at Fort Sumter, a federal fortification in the harbor. The Union soldiers in the fort had refused to surrender to Confederate forces, and now they were under attack. Although no Union soldiers died in the battle, the incident was considered the starting point of the Civil War.

Many Union supporters were overly confident that the war would end almost before it started. For her part, Clara believed in the righteousness of a Union victory, but she was not so bold as to predict a timetable for the outcome. She was also determined to help out in whatever way possible. "I think the city will be attacked within the next 60 days. If it must be, let it come, and when there is no longer a soldier's arm to raise the Stars and Stripes above our Capitol, may God give strength to mine."

Her first opportunity came sooner than she imagined. A regiment of troops from Massachusetts had arrived by train in Baltimore. There, they were supposed to move from one station to another for the trip to Washington. As they marched through the streets, a crowd of Southern sympathizers attacked them. In the unforeseen skirmish, several soldiers died and others were wounded. Although the rest reached Washington safely, they did so without any of their luggage, which in the confusion had been left behind. Clara later

The news that the union was dissolved spread quickly throughout the North and South.

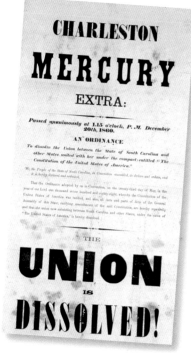

CHARLESTON

MERCURY

EXTRA:

Passed *unanimously* at 1.15 o'clock, P. M. December 20th, 1860.

AN ORDINANCE

To dissolve the Union between the State of South Carolina and other States united with her under the compact entitled "The Constitution of the United States of America."

THE

UNION
IS
DISSOLVED!

Southern sympathizers attacked soldiers from Massachusetts, who were on their way to battle.

reported that the new soldiers had "nothing but their heavy woolen clothes—not a cotton shirt, and many of them not even a pocket handkerchief."

Clara immediately went to work. She packed up as much food and supplies as she could quickly buy or collect from donations, and went to the Capitol where the troops were being temporarily housed. Among the recruits were some of her former students. She was determined that none of the soldiers should ever feel alone or without a friend nearby.

From this improvised beginning, Clara was soon expanding her efforts to equip other troops arriving in Washington with supplies of every kind, supplies that they were unable to obtain through any official channels. The suddenness of the war had rudely displayed the nation's lack of preparation for dealing with prolonged hostilities. Doctors and nurses were few in number, and basic medicine and bandages were hard to come by. There was no shortage of ways Clara could help. "Our armies cannot afford that our ladies lay down their needles and fold their hands; if their contributions are not needed just today, they may be tomorrow . . ."

Over time the situation improved, but this only underscored other needs. After the Union lost the First Battle of Bull Run in July 1861, it became clear that the war was not going to end quickly. Helping soldiers in hospitals was important, but it wasn't going to be enough. Wounded soldiers needed proper treatment as soon as possible, even on the battlefield.

But improving the woeful state of medical care on the battlefield would not be easy. The Union army had fewer than 100 doctors when the war began (they would employ thousands before the war ended), and even established doctors rarely had any formal medical training. They had often served apprenticeships under older doctors, a haphazard process that led to uneven levels of experience. Their tools were basic, consisting of various scalpels, saws, forceps, and scissors. Ether was available

The limited medical supplies available during battles were not much help with severe injuries.

ANESTHESIA

Anesthesia is the loss of feeling or consciousness from the administration of a drug designed to induce this effect.

as an anesthesia, and morphine and liquor were also used to dull pain.

If these had been their only hurdles, they might still have overcome them. But the biggest and most deadly problem was germs—because nobody knew they existed. Doctors would go from patient to patient without washing their hands or their instruments in between.

Diseases such as typhoid, pneumonia, and dysentery spread easily in these conditions. At least as many soldiers died due to the unhealthy conditions in field hospitals as from wounds received on the battlefield. Even without medical training, Clara knew

Field hospitals were little more than tents with cots, and they usually lacked the space to house all the wounded.

Clara returned home during the war to be with her father, Stephen, before he died.

how precarious the life of a wounded soldier could be. Clearly, if injuries could be treated more quickly, more soldiers would survive. But here she faced a personal hurdle: Respectable women were never seen anywhere near a battlefield. The only women who followed soldiers around were disreputable ones looking to provide the army with social and other comforts. "I struggled long and hard with my sense of propriety," Clara wrote later. Her reputation was not something she would part with lightly.

In the midst of this internal debate, she received troubling news from home. Her 88-year-old father was dying, and Clara immediately returned to Massachusetts in the winter of 1862 to nurse him through his final illness. They had long conversations about what she should do upon rejoining the war effort. Her father urged her to do what was right. "Go, if it is your duty to go," advised Captain Barton. "I know soldiers, and they will respect you and your errand."

William A. Hammond (1828–1900) was appointed surgeon general of the United States during the Civil War.

The Second Battle of Bull Run, fought on August 28–30, 1862, was another victory for the Confederacy.

He passed away not long after this, with Clara at his side.

When Clara returned to Washington, she renewed her efforts to bring relief to soldiers on the front. After months of trying to get permission from the government, Clara was successful. In August 1862, William A. Hammond, surgeon general of the United States, sent Clara a letter she could use to visit the battlefields. This was significant, since no other women were allowed to perform such duties.

"So far as our poor efforts can reach, they shall never lack a kindly hand or a sister's sympathy."

—Clara Barton, in her memoirs

Her first stop was Cedar Mountain, Virginia, about 60 miles from Washington. There, the Union had just lost a battle to Confederate forces under the command of Thomas "Stonewall" Jackson. It was a hectic time. As she later described the experience, Clara spent "five days and nights with three hours' sleep—a narrow escape from capture—and some days of getting the wounded into hospitals" back in Washington.

Clara was still caring for the injured soldiers of Cedar Mountain when the Second Battle of Bull Run began. She immediately put together a team to help out there as well. The volunteers arrived to find 3,000 men in need of assistance. Taking stock of their supplies, Clara found that they had only "two water buckets, five tin cups, one camp kettle, one stewpan, two lanterns, four bread knives, three plates, and a two-quart tin dish . . ." She tended to the wounded all night by candlelight.

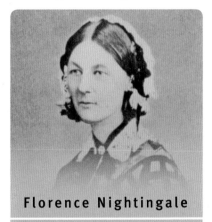

Florence Nightingale

Florence Nightingale (1820-1910), whose life closely mirrored Clara Barton's, was a pioneering British war-time nurse. She arrived in Turkey during the Crimean War and began instituting reforms to improve sanitary conditions and other living conditions in the army. She was known as "The Lady with the Lamp" for her habit of visiting among the wounded soldiers at night.

Both sides suffered heavy losses in the Battle of Antietam, often called the bloodiest battle of the Civil War.

Soon another battle followed nearby, and then another. At the Battle of Chantilly, Clara later recalled staying longer in a dangerous area than was safe on foot. An officer galloped up to her, worried for her safety. The enemy was advancing and would soon overtake her position. Reassured that she could ride a horse, with or without a lady's saddle, the officer told her she could stay another hour.

Two weeks later Clara was at Antietam in Maryland. This was the first battle fought in a Northern state, and it was the bloodiest one of the war. On September 17, 1862, 55,000 men from the Army of the South engaged 75,000 men from the Union's Army of the Potomac in battle. When the dust finally cleared, there were 23,000 dead and wounded soldiers. Clara was the only woman in a group of 30 volunteers. The group was busy, and they did everything from making gruel to wrapping bandages. As the battle raged back and forth across the countryside, the volunteers had to move their makeshift hospital or risk being captured or killed. The constant barrage of artillery shook the earth and fire raged all around. Finally, there was quiet, as the weary men nursed their wounds. The dead were already silent. Victory had been gained and lost and gained again as the Confederate army was eventually repulsed.

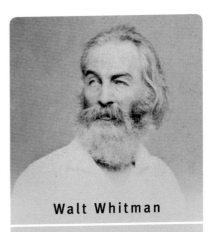

Walt Whitman

Walt Whitman (1819–1892) was an American poet, most famous for writing the collection of poetry called *Leaves of Grass*, which was first published in 1855. During the Civil War, he volunteered as a nurse in Washington, D.C., hospitals and witnessed many of the same scenes as Clara Barton. In 1863, a New York newspaper published an account of his experiences called "The Great Army of the Sick."

After three sleepless days and nights, Clara was exhausted and feverish. She returned to Washington in the back of a wagon and went home to rest.

She didn't get out of bed for a week.

ARTILLERY

Artillery is a large weapon that fires projectiles over short or long distances.

chapter **6**

Lady in Charge

The Union victory at Antietam—or at least its success at dodging a defeat—was a critical moment in the war. Both sides had sustained heavy casualties, but the Union could absorb its losses more readily. Its army was larger, and it had a bigger civilian population to draw on for replacements. The Confederate army under General Robert E. Lee could claim that it had done well considering its disadvantages in terms of men and supplies—but doing well wasn't the same thing as winning. And without clear and decisive victories, the South was on a losing course.

So it was with a sense of renewed hope that President Lincoln reviewed the Union troops in early October 1862.

The Battle of Antietam temporarily halted the Confederate army's march into Union territory.

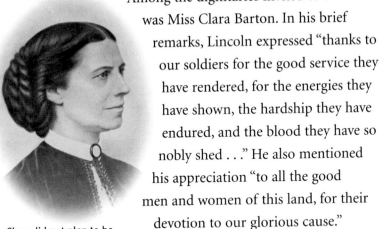

Among the dignitaries invited to attend was Miss Clara Barton. In his brief remarks, Lincoln expressed "thanks to our soldiers for the good service they have rendered, for the energies they have shown, the hardship they have endured, and the blood they have so nobly shed . . ." He also mentioned his appreciation "to all the good men and women of this land, for their devotion to our glorious cause."

Clara did not plan to be involved in the Civil War, but she did pursue opportunities to help out.

Most of the men and women were not known by name. Their deeds remained anonymous. But Clara Barton was an exception. Her time on the battlefield had made her famous. She did not shun the attention, which included a decoration from

the 21st Massachusetts Regiment, which gave her the title, "Daughter of the Regiment." But this was not her main source of satisfaction. Much more

> **REGIMENT**
> A regiment is a military unit, usually consisting of thousands of soldiers.

important were the lives she had saved, using her intellect and her indomitable spirit.

Clara's battlefield experiences had taught her that treating the wounded as soon as possible was critical to keeping their injuries from getting worse. Heroic work was being done by the doctors and nurses in the Washington hospitals, but too many soldiers died before they reached them. Clara wanted to institute a more regular and systematic way to treat soldiers where they fell. Her intention was to serve on the battlefield itself. The reservations she had once held about placing herself in such situations were now banished from her mind.

Clara realized, however, that to take this next step, she would need official support. Luckily, her recent fame proved useful in contacting the quartermaster general, Daniel

Rucker. He put at her command six wagons filled with food, medicine, and other supplies, along with the

The Battle of Fredericksburg was marked by Union losses that were more than twice those of the Confederates.

necessary mules and mule drivers. At first, the men balked at following Clara's orders, but she won them over by sharing their hardships.

The next major confrontation took place at Fredericksburg, Virginia, along the Rappahannock River. It was cold that December, and the freezing temperatures took their toll on North and South alike. On the Fredericksburg side of the river, General Lee commanded 78,000 men. On the opposite side,

General Ambrose Burnside (1824–1881) was remembered for the prominent facial hair named after him: sideburns.

General Ambrose Burnside had an army of 120,000. He made the decision to build a bridge across the river so that his men could engage the enemy on the opposite shore. His hope was to catch Lee unprepared for this move.

This strategy proved to be a disaster. Although the bridge was successfully built, the crossing soldiers were heavily exposed to Confederate fire. Casualties mounted quickly. When the battle was at its peak, a courier gave Clara a note from a "lion-hearted old surgeon" who had established a hospital "in the very jaws of death." The penciled message read: "Come to me. Your place is here."

Ignoring the bullets whizzing by, Clara moved toward the surgeon's position. Artillery shells burst all around her. One

There was a significant chance of Clara being injured or killed as she served wounded soldiers on the battlefield.

exploded so close it tore away part of her dress but left her otherwise unharmed.

The surgeon was glad of her services. He had set up his hospital in an old mansion. Wounded soldiers were draped everywhere—in the bed, on the floor, even on the wide shelves of a cupboard. "Think of trying to lie still and die quietly," Clara wrote, describing what the soldiers were enduring, "lest you fall out of a bed six feet high."

As the battle progressed, Clara found herself treating Confederate as well as Union soldiers. She was later criticized for this action, but she remained steadfast in her opinion that she had done the right thing. All wounded men were human beings who deserved medical care.

At one point, an older veteran officer, unaware of Clara's role, came galloping to her side, thinking she was a refugee from the city. He

Clara wanted wounded soldiers to receive proper care both on the battlefield and in the hospital.

offered her protection, but she declined, though she appreciated his chivalry. At that moment, knowing how much the wounded soldiers nearby appreciated her efforts, she considered herself "the best-protected woman in the United States."

When she finally returned home to Washington, Clara was by her own description, "shoeless, gloveless, ragged and blood-stained." Whatever pride she might later feel in her actions, for the moment she was consumed by "desolation and pity and sympathy and weariness, all blended."

Ulysses S. Grant

Ulysses S. Grant (1822–1885) graduated from the United States Military Academy at West Point in 1843. He had an undistinguished service record for several years and retired from the army in the 1850s to pursue a career in business. At the onset of the Civil War, he rejoined the army and rose to lead it to eventual victory. In 1868, he was elected President of the United States and served for two terms.

By the spring of 1863, she had recovered her strength. With the Army of the Potomac better provisioned, Clara turned her focus further south. She traveled to Hilton Head, South Carolina, and for the next eight months she tended to soldiers during the siege of Charleston (a Union siege that ultimately failed).

Robert E. Lee

Robert E. Lee (1807–1870) was a career army officer who served in several distinguished capacities in the United States Army before the Civil War. President Lincoln asked him to take command of the Union army in early 1861, but he declined out of loyalty to his native state, Virginia. Lee was an inspiring leader of the Confederate army, and after the war he served as president of Washington and Lee University.

The following May, she was called to take part in the Wilderness Campaign. The Union army was now under the overall command of Lieutenant General Ulysses S. Grant. He had recently earned a reputation as a tenacious leader. Having been disappointed in the leadership of one Union general after another, President Lincoln hoped Grant would prove to be up to the task.

Grant began by chasing Lee and his army across a densely forested area southwest of Washington. In such a setting, Grant could not make the best use of his larger force, and Lee claimed several victories. Unlike his predecessors, however, Grant did not retreat or even settle for holding his ground in the face of defeat. He simply attacked again. And again. Given his superior numbers of men and supplies, Grant could afford to lose battles as long as the South incurred heavy losses in their victories—losses they were ill-prepared to absorb. This strategy, though it led to many deaths on both sides, finally changed the momentum of the war.

At the end of June 1864, Clara was made superintendent of the Department of Nurses for the army massed along the James River in Virginia. As the lady in charge, she reported to General Benjamin Butler, who was one of her strongest supporters. His standing order to his men was to "honor any request that Miss Barton makes without question. She out-ranks me." Not every death under her care was dramatic. In one hospital ward, Clara remembered, "I stopped beside a black sergeant who had appeared weak all day, but made no complaint, and asked how he was feeling then. Looking up at my face, he replied, 'Thank you, Miss, a little better, I hope.' 'Can I do anything for you?' I asked. 'A little water, if you please.' I turned to get it, and that instant he gasped and was gone."

The battles continued, but a hint of desperation had crept into the Southern ranks. Short of troops, Lee had to abandon long-held positions near Richmond, Virginia. Through the fall of 1864 and the winter of 1865, the Confederate army suffered a

General Benjamin Butler (1818–1893) followed his service in the Civil War by serving as a member of Congress.

Generals Grant and Lee met in the home of the MacLean family, which was originally built as a tavern in 1848.

series of setbacks. Richmond, the Confederate capital, finally fell on April 3, 1865. Lee considered a retreat that would gather his scattered forces in the mountains, but he lacked the support for even that journey. On April 9, he surrendered to Grant in a farmhouse at Appomattox, Virginia. The Civil War was over.

Clara shared in the country's joy. She also agreed with the sentiments that President Lincoln had expressed the month before in his second inaugural address: "With malice toward none, with charity for all . . . let us strive on to finish the work we are in; to bind up the nation's wounds."

Clara had already taken her own step to "bind up the nation's wounds." Her reputation for helping Union soldiers had prompted many people to write her inquiring about friends and family who had gone missing during the fighting. Most presumably had died in prisoner-of-war camps. But what exactly had become of them and where were their remains? Any information that Clara could provide would be much appreciated.

In response to her request, President Lincoln had officially authorized Clara to set up a National Register to resolve as many of these mysteries as possible. On March 11, 1865, President Lincoln had composed a letter, writing: "To the Friends of Missing Persons: Miss Clara Barton has kindly offered to search for the missing prisoners of war. Please address her at Annapolis, giving her the name, regiment, and company of any missing prisoner."

It was one of Lincoln's last official acts. Only five days after Appomattox, the president was shot while attending a play. Lincoln died early the next morning, leaving the nation in a state of shock and dismay. The work of reuniting the country would continue, but the joy in doing it would be greatly lessened.

Meanwhile, Clara embarked on her latest challenge. The task she faced was immense. Almost 150,000 Northern soldiers had been buried in unidentified graves, and more than 40,000 other deaths had been recorded with

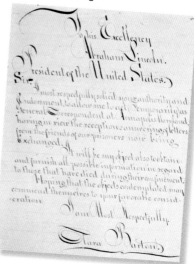

In this letter, Clara asks President Lincoln for the the authority to search for missing soldiers.

Dorence Atwater (1845–1910) followed his time with Clara by serving abroad as a consul in Tahiti.

no evidence of what had happened to the bodies. She could make inquiries, she could investigate, but there was no certainty of success. Fortunately, a young soldier, Dorence Atwater, heard of her mission and came to see her. An army private, he had been captured in July 1863 and sent to the newly opened prison in Andersonville, Georgia. Andersonville had earned the reputation of being the worst of the Confederate prisons. Thousands of Union prisoners had died behind its walls. Atwater had been given the job of compiling a death list, and he had made a secret copy, believing that the original would never reach the proper federal authorities. He now planned to publish the list of almost 13,000 men, but first he wanted Clara Barton to see it.

Clara took Atwater to Andersonville along with 42 headboard carvers. The scene was chilling, even though the prison was no longer operating. Of Andersonville, she said: "I have looked over its 25 acres of pitiless stockade, its burrows in the earth, its stinted stream, its turfless hillside, shadeless in summer and shelterless in winter; its well, and tunnels and graves, its seven forts of death, its ball and chains, its stocks and tortures . . . My heart went out and I said,

> ## *"'Surely this was not the gate of hell, but hell itself . . ."*
>
> —Clara Barton, in her memoirs

'Surely this was not the gate of hell, but hell itself . . .'"

At Andersonville, Clara and her helpers set up a new national cemetery and were able to identify most of the remains over the next few years. Clara received more than 60,000 letters during this time, and she did her best to investigate every missing person she could. Before she had finished, 20,000 men were found.

With this work finished, Clara could put the Civil War behind her.

Andersonville Cemetery remains a sober reminder of the prison where thousands of people died.

chapter **7**

Speaking Her Mind

The nation was still exhausted. Thousands of families on both sides continued to mourn the loss of fallen soldiers. Lives had been shattered, homes burned, and land ruined. In the South, where most of the fighting had taken place, the government itself needed to be rebuilt as well.

However, any construction would have to take place without the aid of slaves. The process of ending slavery had begun with Lincoln's Emancipation Proclamation in January 1863, which had declared slaves in the Confederate states to be free. The end of the war freed more slaves, but

this event was not enough to change the minds of people who still considered African-Americans to be an inferior race. These individuals were determined to keep blacks "in their place," unable to vote or own

The Emancipation Proclamation was the first major step taken toward freeing the slaves in the United States.

Freed slaves faced the challenge of starting new lives without an education or financial support.

property. Even if blacks could not be called slaves, they could still be denied any real power in society. If that goal was achieved, their situation might not be much improved.

To guard against this outcome, three new amendments to the Constitution were passed. The first, the Thirteenth Amendment, stated that "neither slavery nor involuntary servitude . . . shall exist within the United States, or any place subject to their jurisdiction." The second, the Fourteenth Amendment, made sure that it was understood that blacks were citizens of the United States. And the third, the Fifteenth Amendment, built on the others by declaring that the "right of citizens of the United States to vote shall not be denied or abridged by the United States or by any State on account of race, color, or previous condition of servitude." Although these amendments were clear in their intent, prejudice continued to hold sway in some states, and often found new ways to express itself.

AMENDMENT

An amendment is a permanent change to an existing document, such as the United States Constitution.

Many former slaves continued to work as sharecroppers on or near the plantations where they had been slaves.

Clara Barton agreed with the sentiments underlying the amendments. Her parents had been abolitionists, part of the movement to end slavery that had risen in the early 19th century. Because of this, she had been raised to believe that blacks should be free. And Clara herself, in traveling during the war, had seen the poor conditions in which many Southern slaves lived. Ending slavery, for her, was the proper thing to do.

Clara had some occasion to voice these sentiments in a new role she had taken on for herself: She started traveling the county and giving lectures. But she had never liked public speaking. Certainly, being a teacher for so many years had helped a little, but addressing a familiar group of students every day was not the same as speaking to hundreds of strangers in a packed lecture hall.

Yet the fund-raising opportunity to share her war experiences was too valuable to resist. The money being used to identify the remaining missing soldiers had come partly from her own savings, which needed to be replenished. (Congress later awarded her a $15,000 reimbursement for her expenses and personal contributions.)

Clara toured throughout the northeast and the Midwest—visiting Philadelphia, New York, Boston, Chicago, and many smaller cities as well. She once did as many as fourteen lectures in a single month. She did not visit the South, though, where she assumed that her perspective would not be welcome.

Whatever her fears, Clara was quite successful on the lecture circuit. One Peoria, Illinois, newspaper account from December 6, 1867, summed up her appeal. It described her unassuming appearance, which extended from her quiet manner to her conservative black silk dress. Nevertheless, her clear voice rang out. It had the power to make the scenes she described seem immediate and alive. People left her talks feeling that they too had walked the

> I was strong ~ and I thought I ought to go to the rescue of the men who fell ~:
> But I struggled long and hard with my sense of propriety ~ with the appalling fact ~ that I was only a woman, whispering in one ear ~ and the groans of suffering men, dying like dogs ~ unfed and unsheltered, for the life of the very Institutions which had protected and educated me ~ thundering in the other ~.
> ——— I said that I struggled with my sense of propriety ~ and I say it with humiliation and shame ~. Before God and before you I am ashamed that I thought of such a thing ~
> But when our armies fought at Cedar Mountain I broke the shackles and went to the field

Clara read from prepared speeches, but she chose her words to sound informal and conversational.

battlefields with the cannons booming around them.

Although she knew that her audiences wished to hear about her exploits on the battlefield, Clara never glorified the accounts. History, she pointed out, paid little attention to those like herself, who followed in the wake of bloody conflict. She would often recount how she had been told that "women don't know anything about war." Her response to the comment was both eloquent and pointed: "I wish men didn't, either. They have always known a great deal too much about it for the good of their kind."

Among those pleased by Clara's success was the women's rights leader, Susan B. Anthony. She realized that Clara Barton occupied a unique place in public life. Other women could and did speak eloquently of the need for women to be treated fairly and equally. But not every man believed that women deserved this treatment. Through her work during the war, Clara Barton had

Susan B. Anthony (1820–1906) would emerge as one of the most forceful advocates of women's rights.

Men "have always known a great deal too much about [war] for the good of their kind."

—Clara Barton, in her lectures

succeeded as well as any man in the most trying of circumstances. She had proved herself in a way that many women were capable of, but

few, if any, had a chance to demonstrate. Therefore, many men listened to her with a respect they would not give to other women.

But Clara didn't see herself as special. From her perspective, she had simply done the right thing at the time when it was needed. So she was furious one day when she discovered that her appearance at an event in Iowa was being promoted in decided contrast to a speech a suffragette might offer. "Miss Barton does not belong to that class of woman," read the placard advertising her arrival.

The American women's rights movement, launched in 1848, gradually gained strength throughout the 19th century.

After finishing her usual talk, Clara spoke plainly to the

Advancement of Women's Rights

The American fight for women's rights was launched in Seneca Falls, New York, at a convention in 1848. Many of the movement's most famous early leaders, including Elizabeth Cady Stanton and Lucretia Mott, were in attendence at the convention. Prominent among their proposals was the idea that women should have the right to vote. Women finally did gain the right to vote 72 years later, when the twentieth Amendment to the Constitution was ratified in 1919.

audience. She had never forgotten being denied the position of principal in New Jersey. It was an injustice that still rankled her. Such an advertisement, she declared, "does worse than misrepresent me as a woman; it maligns my friend. It abuses the highest and bravest work ever done in this land for you or me." How could they praise her and sneer at the others? Susan B. Anthony, Elizabeth Cady Stanton, Frances D. Gage, and the rest had persevered over years of resistance to insist that a woman had "the right to her own property; her own children; her own home, her just individual claim before the law, to her freedom of action, to her personal liberty." Clara wholeheartedly applauded their work. Her personal path may have taken her in a different direction, but that should not lessen their accomplishments. She then raised a cheer for Susan B. Anthony, and the crowd followed her lead.

Although Clara's current work lacked the dangers of the war years, it was tiring nonetheless and took a toll on her health. One winter night in 1868, she was speaking in

Portland, Maine, with no forewarning of what was to come. And then "gradually to my horror I felt my voice giving out, leaving me. The next moment I opened my mouth but no sound followed. Again and again I attempted it, with no result. It was finished!"

Since she was unable to speak, she canceled the rest of her tour. She wrote to Elizabeth Cady Stanton and Susan B. Anthony that the "years of unsheltered days and nights, the sun and storm, the dews and damps have done their work and now with bitter tears, I turn my face away from the land I have loved so well and seek in a foreign clime, perchance a little of the good strength once lent me here."

Elizabeth Cady Stanton (1815–1902) was an abolitionist before she became one of the early leaders of the women's rights movement.

Her doctor had recommended that she travel abroad to recuperate. "You can't rest in your own country," he told her. "They won't let you."

Clara knew herself well enough to realize the doctor was right. She decided to take his advice.

Frances D. Gage (1808–1884) was active in the women's rights movements, focusing on the right to vote.

chapter **8**

Travels Abroad

When Clara sailed for Europe in 1869, she had few thoughts about her long-term future. Restoring her health was her main priority. She began the trip touring in Scotland and England, and continued on to Geneva, Switzerland, for a longer stay with the parents of a friend. While she was there, a group of prominent Swiss citizens came to see her. They had heard of Miss Barton's work in the Civil War and wanted to share their own experiences with her.

One story they told her involved a Swiss businessman named Henry Dunant. Ten years earlier, in June 1859, he had been traveling on the Italian peninsula, where he witnessed the

Geneva, Switzerland, with its central European location, has a reputation for political and diplomatic neutrality.

aftermath of a 16-hour battle between French and Austrian forces. At day's end, as Clara later recounted, "sixteen thousand French and Sardinian soldiers and twenty thousand Austrians lay dead or were wounded and disabled on that field . . . For days after the battle the dead in part remained unburied, and the wounded where they fell, or crawled away as they could for shelter and help." Dunant was both greatly moved and greatly appalled by the sight. He was not concerned with who had started the war, or who was right or wrong. What concerned him was the inhumane treatment the wounded had received.

Henry Dunant

Henry Dunant (1828–1910) came from a religious family that stressed social work. Although he participated in several organizations that helped the poor, he started his adult life working at an ordinary bank job. However, after helping to start the International Red Cross, he devoted much of his time to pursuing his ideals at the expense of financial success. In 1901, he shared the first Nobel Peace Prize for his work in establishing the International Red Cross and the Geneva Conventions.

Dunant was so affected that he recorded this and other experiences in a book, *A Memory of Soferino.* In its pages he argued for the more humane and effective treatment of wounded soldiers. Most notably, he asked this question: "Would it not be possible to found and organize in all

> *"Would it not be possible to found and organize in all civilized countries volunteers which in time of war would reendow succor to the wounded without distinction of nationality?"*
>
> —Henry Dunant, in *A Memory of Soferino*

civilized countries volunteers which in time of war would reendow succor to the wounded without distinction of nationality?"

In 1863, with the support of wealthy benefactors, Dunant founded the International Committee of the Red Cross. The flag of Switzerland features a white cross on a red field, and because of its origins in that country, the Red Cross took as its symbol the reverse of the Swiss flag—a red cross on a white background.

A year later, the first Geneva Convention was held. Its purpose was to create a set of rules regarding the care of wounded soldiers that would govern all countries during wartime. The Red Cross would handle the care if the countries involved in the fighting abided by its guidelines. One such guideline was that Red Cross workers would be considered neutral in any conflict. In practical terms, this meant they would not be shot at. They would also not be subject to capture or

BENEFACTOR

A benefactor is a wealthy person who gives money to worthy causes.

imprisonment by either side. And their medical supplies would remain under their direct control and not be removed for any reason.

Clara hadn't heard about this before coming to Europe. Adding to her surprise, she learned that 31 countries had already subscribed to the

This design became the official flag of the Red Cross in 1863.

Geneva Convention, "with one great and incomprehensible exception, the United States of America."

Given her success in enlisting government aid during the Civil War, Clara was puzzled by her country's reluctance to participate. As it turned out, the problem was that the United States had a longstanding desire to stay out of any European treaties. In his Farewell Address in 1796, George Washington had warned the country to avoid foreign entanglements, "to steer clear of permanent alliances with any portion of the foreign world." The Monroe Doctrine of 1823 stated flatly that European countries should not colonize lands or interfere with the affairs of existing countries in the Western Hemisphere. By extension, the United States would stay out of European matters. On the surface, the Geneva Convention looked like something for America to avoid on principle.

And that's where the situation rested. Secretary of state William H. Seward, who served under presidents Lincoln and Johnson, was opposed to the idea of agreeing to the Geneva Convention, and so was his successor, Hamilton Fish.

William H. Seward (1801–1872) had a long and distinguished political career.

There was also the problematic fact that many European governments had been sympathetic to the Confederate states during the Civil War, and the Union government was not quite ready to forgive them.

Despite these seeming justifications, Clara was not satisfied. "I began to fear that in the eyes of the rest of mankind we could not be far from barbarians," she later wrote. "This reflection did not furnish a stimulating food for national pride. I grew more and more ashamed." It was her belief that American reluctance came from a condition of ignorance more than anything else. After all, if she herself had been unfamiliar with the Red Cross, she could hardly blame the American public for being similarly uninformed.

On July 15, 1870, a few months after Clara's arrival in

> *"I began to fear that in the eyes of the rest of mankind we could not be far from barbarians. This reflection did not furnish a stimulating food for national pride. I grew more and more ashamed."*
>
> —Clara Barton, in her memoirs

Europe, a war (later known as the Franco-Prussian War) broke out between France and the German state of Prussia. They were fighting over who should rule Spain, where the throne was currently vacant (a post that the Spanish apparently were not able to fill themselves). The Prussians were naturally hoping to install a German candidate, an idea the French just as naturally opposed, since this would mean facing German rulers on two of their borders.

Whatever their reasons for fighting, both France and Prussia had agreed to the Geneva Convention. Therefore they allowed representatives from the Red Cross to proceed to the front and take charge

During the Franco-Prussian War, the Prussians defeated the French after only 10 months in May, 1871.

In temporary military hospitals like this one, aid workers were able to tend to the wounded.

of the wounded. The war lasted a grueling 10 months, and the Red Cross was very busy during that time. The 400,000 soldiers in the French army were facing a force led by Prussia, but including other German states, making it almost three times as large. In addition, the Prussian forces were better trained and better supplied than the French army.

Although the Germans dominated the fighting, there were numerous casualties on both sides. At first, Clara wasn't well enough to help out on the battlefields, but she still went to observe and marvel at what the Red Cross was able to accomplish. Its operations lay in stark contrast to her memories of the Civil War. Despite her successes, she remembered battles with their "starving wounded, frozen to the ground, and our commission and their supplies in Washington" unable to reach them. One battle, the Siege of Petersburg, had left "4,000 dead and wounded and no flag of truce, the wounded broiling in a July sun, dying and rotting where they fell."

The Red Cross, with its clear international mandate, managed

MANDATE

A mandate is an order to be fulfilled by a person or organization.

things better. As Clara wrote, "I saw the work of these Red Cross societies in the field accomplishing in four months . . . what we failed to accomplish in four years . . . no mistakes, no needless suffering, no waste, no confusion, but order, plenty, cleanliness, and comfort . . . I said to myself, 'if I live to return to my country, I will try to make my people understand the Red Cross and that treaty.'"

As Clara became more involved with the relief efforts, she made friends with the Grand Duchess Louise of Baden, the daughter of the Prussian King Wilhelm I. Her mother, Queen Augusta, was the head of the Red Cross in Prussia. With the Grand Duchess's help, Clara toured hospitals and distributed much needed supplies. In particular, she made her presence felt in Strasbourg, a French city on the Prussian border that had just fallen under German control. The fighting in and around Strasbourg had left perhaps 20,000 people homeless, with no immediate way to care for themselves.

Grand Duchess Louise of Baden (1838–1923) was a humanitarian and the only daughter of Wilhelm I of Germany.

Clara soon wrote a letter to the prime minister of Prussia, Otto von Bismarck, explaining her plan. She had noted the French bitterness against the German invaders and sought

Otto von Bismarck (1815–1898) became the first Chancellor of Germany and advocated a balance-of-power approach.

to lessen it, if possible. She intended to do this by making sure that the Germans got the credit for any assistance or charity the French population received.

In addition, rather than simply giving people help until supplies ran out, Clara fostered a new idea. She set up "Workrooms for Women," small shops where women could sew clothing for sale to people who needed it. This way, instead of merely assisting displaced people, she was putting some of them back to work. Always, she sought to emphasize that the Germans had made this possible. As she explained in a letter: "This population must always be the neighbors, if not a part of, the German people; it will be most desirable that they should be also friends; they are in distress—their hearts can never be better reached than now; the little seeds of today may have in it the germs of future peace or war."

In other parts of France Clara introduced a similar system, giving women the opportunity to make and sell clothes to those in need. Her interest in clothing was not dictated by fashion. The clothes of many people in war-torn areas were riddled with disease and bugs, and she hoped the new clothing would give them a fresh start. Otherwise, many of those who survived the fighting were bound to fall victim to disease in the months or years to come.

Although the war ended in May 1871, the demands on Clara's schedule brought on a recurrence of her poor health. She had received several honors for her recent work, but they could not brighten her mood for long. She tried traveling again to raise her spirits, but Paris only cheered her a little, and she spent a less than happy winter in London in 1873.

She might not have been well, but she was still able to move about. In October, she boarded a ship and returned to America.

The Workrooms for Women restored a sense of pride in the women who participated.

chapter **9**

The American Red Cross

Clara Barton returned home to a United States that was not in the best of spirits. A financial panic had struck the country only a couple of weeks earlier. The speculative boom that had accompanied the end of the Civil War had suddenly collapsed with devastating effect. Many banks were failing, and business stocks had fallen sharply as well. Wage cuts and job losses quickly followed.

None of this affected Clara's personal finances directly, but it was not the best time to promote a new international agency like the Red Cross. And in her weakened condition, she was unable to pursue any causes, however noble. As she later recalled, "Only a small portion of the time could I stand alone; averaged less than two hours' sleep in 24 for almost a year; could not write my name for over four months, and could

> *"I have in these exhausted days only a given amount of strength, and if, by accident or oversight, I overdraw my account, I am at once bankrupt, and can carry on business no further."*
>
> —Clara Barton, in her memoirs

The famous writer Mark Twain was one of the early, high-profile proponents of the manual typewriter.

not have a letter read to me or see my friends or scarcely my attendants." The only time she left home was to return to Oxford because her sister Sally was dying.

Over the next two years, her situation scarcely improved. It was hard to believe, especially for Clara herself, that the same person who had endured wartime hardships for weeks on end could become so physically hampered. And yet she seemed helpless to break out of her weakened state. "I have in these exhausted days only a given amount of strength," she wrote, "and if, by accident or oversight, I overdraw my account, I am at once bankrupt, and can carry on business no further."

As patriotic as Clara was, she didn't have the energy to attend the 1876 Centennial Exposition in Philadelphia. This celebration of the 100th anniversary of the nation's independence featured such exhibits as the right arm and torch of a proposed Statue of Liberty to be built in New York Harbor. The exposition also featured new inventions, such as the typewriter and the telephone.

Clara decided that she needed to shake things up and change her surroundings to give herself a chance to get better. That summer,

SANITARIUM

A sanitarium is a medical institution designed for patients whose needs require long-term care.

she moved to a sanitarium in Dansville, New York, where her condition improved. "I have done everything to surround myself with healthful and strength-giving influences," she wrote. "The climate is delicious and I almost live in the open air. Sleep, which in all years has been only a visitor, has come back to bide with me more constantly. My flesh is also returning and I am regaining some powers of endurance."

As her slow recovery continued, Clara retained an unassuming honesty and sense of humor about herself. When one prospective visitor inquired about the chance of visiting her, she advised him not to get his hopes up about her physical appearance. She had no illusions about her looks. "I was never what the world calls even good-looking, leaving out of the case all such terms as 'handsome' and

'pretty.'" Her best feature, she believed, had been her dark hair which had long since turned gray.

Dansville, New York, was later the site of one of the first chapters of the American Red Cross.

When the time came to leave the sanitarium, Clara bought a house nearby so that she could remain in Dansville. There, she finally regained enough strength to think again about bringing the Red Cross to America. In 1877, she sought advice from Dr. Louis Appia, a Swiss surgeon who had helped found the International Red Cross. He was very glad to hear from her after a silence of several years. And he had some very specific suggestions concerning the shape her campaign should take.

Rutherford B. Hayes (1822–1893) became president in 1876 after one of the closest elections in American history.

First, she had to "awaken the attention, the sympathy, and the confidence of the public. Without the public, no money, and without money no material help." She also had to find a way to meet with President Rutherford B. Hayes. Without his support, no plan would succeed. She also had to detail a practical way to mount relief efforts to other countries. In fact, Dr. Appia hoped that progress could be made quickly enough to launch a relief effort to help out in the current war between Russia and Turkey. As dedicated as she was, Clara doubted she could manage anything that fast.

Her biggest adversary was ignorance. It was important to get everyone in the government to understand the mission of the Red Cross. The Geneva Convention was not a military treaty. It was not an obligation that would drag a reluctant country into war. The Red Cross was a humanitarian organization whose only goal was to alleviate suffering on the battlefield and elsewhere.

To promote this point, she created a pamphlet describing the ideas and principles that embodied the Red Cross. She explained that while the efforts of volunteers and others (including herself) were both noble and helpful, they were generally insufficient to deal with the nightmares that war created. The Geneva Convention was not a society, something that the United States would need to belong to, but rather "a treaty under which all the relief societies of the Red Cross are enabled to carry on their work effectually." Since those societies would be universally recognized,

The work of the Geneva Convention fostered the idea of peaceful cooperation between countries.

there would be no confusion about their role or authority in their accepted domain. But the Red Cross would not be limited to battlefields: "Organized in every State, the relief societies of the Red Cross would be ready with money, nurses, and supplies to go on call to the instant relief of all who were overwhelmed by any of the sudden calamities that occasionally visit us." Another strength of the organization would be its constant readiness. Instead

Clara Barton was both stubborn and patient in her pursuit of American support for the Red Cross.

of pulling together a hodgepodge of rescue services at a moment's notice, the Red Cross would always be organized and prepared to face an emergency head-on.

As logical as this proposal may have seemed to Clara, it was not immediately successful. Clara was able to meet with President Hayes in 1877. He was cordial, but passed her request like a baton to the secretary of state, who in turn passed it to the assistant secretary of state. Unfortunately, the assistant secretary of state, Frederick Seward, was the son of William H. Seward, Lincoln's secretary of state, and he remembered his father's disapproval of the idea. As far as the younger Seward was concerned, nothing had changed.

It was understandable, perhaps, that a son didn't want to overrule his father, but that was no consolation. Clara didn't do much better when she approached members of Congress. She had some supporters, but the rest were either not interested in listening or misunderstood her intent. America didn't need a bunch of foreigners telling them what to do in hard times or, even worse, ordering them around in a crisis.

Under the circumstances, Clara might have retreated in defeat. But she hadn't lived in Washington for so many years without learning a few things. One of them was that in politics, nothing lasts forever. So she waited. And to help things along, she campaigned for the Democratic presidential

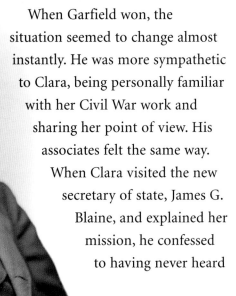

Frederick W. Seward (1830–1915) was assistant secretary of state during and after the Civil War.

nominee in 1880, Ohio congressman James A. Garfield.

When Garfield won, the situation seemed to change almost instantly. He was more sympathetic to Clara, being personally familiar with her Civil War work and sharing her point of view. His associates felt the same way. When Clara visited the new secretary of state, James G. Blaine, and explained her mission, he confessed to having never heard of the Red Cross. Clara offered to give him a full explanation if he had the time. "Miss Barton," he replied, "I can give you all the time you need." As Clara made her case, Blaine asked why such a straightforward matter had not been previously resolved. She explained that the younger Seward had deferred to the older Seward's notion that the Red Cross would infringe on the tenets of the Monroe Doctrine. To this, Secretary Blaine

James G. Blaine (1830–1893) lost the presidential election of 1884 to Democratic candidate, Grover Cleveland.

promptly replied that "the Monroe Doctrine was not made to ward off humanity."

After that, Clara visited other officials and found them equally receptive. Suddenly, the idea of an American Red Cross made all the sense in the world. Clara could hardly believe it. She was intent on seizing the moment, and on May 21, 1881, a little over two months after Garfield took office, a meeting of the American Red Cross met for the first time. The United States was not yet a signee of the Geneva Convention treaty, but surely that would happen soon.

James A. Garfield (1831–1881) served as a Civil War general, as well as in Congress, before being elected president.

Given the pattern established in other countries, it would have been appropriate for President Garfield to lead the American Red Cross. But he refused, telling Clara that she should be the president.

And then the unexpected happened. On July 2, 1881, President Garfield was shot in a Washington train station. The nation was shocked at the possibility of the second assassination in 16 years. The president lingered for 80 days, and during that time any official Red Cross recognition remained in limbo.

But Clara herself was very busy. In early September, a huge fire started in eastern Michigan, leaving farms and businesses in ruins and 5,000 people homeless. Clara marshaled several new Red Cross chapters to help with the disaster. She led the relief effort herself, and donated money for much-needed supplies. The scene when she arrived was devastating. "Our skies grew murky and dark," she recalled, "and our atmosphere bitter with the drifting smoke that rolled over the blazing fields. Living thousands fled in terror, dying hundreds writhed in the embers, the dead blackened in the ashes of their hard-earned homes."

But she was heartened to be there in a new official capacity, one in which she "felt the help and strength of our organization, young and untried as it was."

After Garfield's death, his successor, Chester A. Arthur, continued to support the Red Cross. But there were inevitable delays as one administration gave way to the next. Finally, in March 1882, President Arthur signed the treaty, and in July it was ratified on the European end. On that occasion, the president of the International Red Cross, Gustave Moynier, publicly thanked Clara for her "energy and perseverance."

For once, Clara could relax and enjoy the moment. "Our adhesion to this treaty has changed our articles of war and our military hospital flag. We have no longer the old faded yellow flag, but a bright Red Cross at every post . . ." Americans were now "not only in full accord with the International Treaty of Geneva but are considered one of the strongest pledged nations within it."

As president, Chester A. Arthur (1829–1886) was an advocate of civil service reform.

chapter **10**

Helping Out All Over

For most Americans, the creation of the American Red Cross was cause for neither joy nor alarm—because they were unaware it had happened. No bold headlines blazed across the newspapers; no feature stories or proud editorials filled the inside pages. In only a few papers did the news show up anywhere at all.

But that would soon change. Michigan had been a first step for the Red Cross, but soon spring floods raged along the Mississippi and Ohio Rivers. In 1884, Clara went to Cincinnati, Ohio, to take charge of the flood-relief efforts there. She chartered a boat to move supplies to stranded residents.

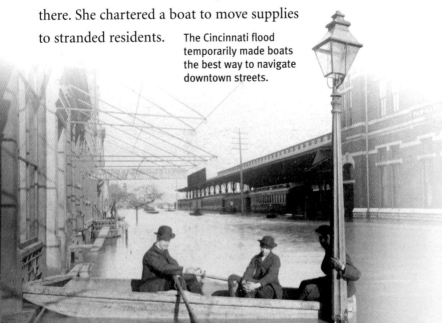

The Cincinnati flood temporarily made boats the best way to navigate downtown streets.

A crew of carpenters was hired to build a series of one-room buildings along the river at various intervals. Each of these new buildings was then loaded with food, clothing, and other necessities to be distributed to local inhabitants.

"The day is not far distant—if it has not already come—when the American people will recognize the Red Cross as one of the wisest and best systems of philanthropic work in modern times."

—Editorial in the Chicago *Inter-Ocean*

These actions did not go unnoticed. On March 31, 1884, one Chicago newspaper editorial proclaimed: "The day is not far distant—if it has not already come—when the American people will recognize the Red Cross as one of the wisest and best systems of philanthropic work in modern times." As Clara noted when reflecting on their efforts, Red Cross volunteers had journeyed up and down the Ohio River and done the same on the Mississippi from St. Louis to New Orleans. In all, they had spent four months traveling more than 8,000 miles.

At 62, an age when many people would be winding down their business activities and looking forward to retirement, Clara Barton was doing just the opposite. Her next assignment was to represent the United States at an International Red Cross conference in Geneva in September 1884. Initially, she had declined to go, feeling tired from her months living along the river. But Secretary of State Blaine insisted that no one else was so qualified to be the American representative. Eventually, she bowed to his insistence.

As the only fully participating female representative, Clara naturally received a great deal of attention at the conference. And since she knew she had earned the right to be there, she was comfortable in the spotlight. The conference went on for a week, dividing its time between organizational issues and demonstrations of new medical techniques and improved equipment. Clara, however, did not hurry home afterward. She stayed in Europe for two months, visiting friends and attending other meetings. She also collected awards and medals from several governments that were eager to honor her.

When Clara did return home, there was much to do. Remembering the slow pace of government bureaucracy, Clara worked to make the American Red Cross as nimble as possible. Neither she nor her aides were paid a salary. Certain sums of money always remained available, not even tucked away in a bank. That way, they would be accessible in any emergency on a moment's notice (even at night or on weekends, when a bank would be closed).

The city of Geneva was a picturesque backdrop for the proceedings at the international conference.

Of course, those funds would not appear by magic. Clara's own financial resources were not unlimited, even if she was willing to commit them as needed. The Red Cross needed to raise money from businesses and individuals. It helped, of course, that it was now receiving positive publicity. Over the next few years, the Red Cross stepped in after a famine in Texas, an earthquake in Charleston, a tornado in Illinois, and a yellow fever outbreak in Florida.

This medal for humanitarian relief work bears the inscription: "God Bless the Red Cross."

Each of these crises was significant, but they paled in comparison to the next one. Several miles north of Johnstown, Pennsylvania, stood the South Fork Dam. After torrential rains in May 1889, the dam burst. Without warning, 20 million tons of water roared downstream, washing away parts of several small towns. But the real damage came in Johnstown. A wall of water 60 feet high—carrying with it trees, houses, and other debris—hit the town while traveling at 40 miles per hour. More than 2,000 people, many of them caught by surprise, died in the initial onslaught; 1,600 homes were destroyed in an area of four square miles.

Sadly, the first call for help was for coffins and undertakers. A few days later, Clara and the Red Cross

YELLOW FEVER

Yellow fever is a virus often spread by mosquitoes. Mild cases last only days, but serious ones can lead to death.

arrived. She never forgot what that first day was like: "The wading in mud, the climbing over broken engines, heaps of iron rollers, broken timbers, wrecks of houses; bent railway tracks tangled with piles of iron wire . . . dead animals and often people borne away."

The Red Cross volunteers set up feeding stations and built a warehouse to store supplies that were coming in from across the country. They also built a series of shelters, known as Red Cross Hotels, to house those who had lost their homes. It took months to restore the area to some semblance of normality. And the Red Cross was there the whole time,

The Johnstown flood left a tremendous amount of trash, debris, and destruction in its wake.

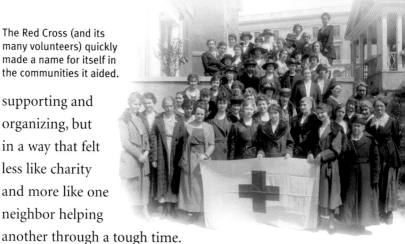

The Red Cross (and its many volunteers) quickly made a name for itself in the communities it aided.

supporting and organizing, but in a way that felt less like charity and more like one neighbor helping another through a tough time.

As rewarding as it was to assist in American emergencies, the mission of the Red Cross was always international in scope. When news reached America in 1891 that more than a million Russians were suffering through a devastating famine, the Red Cross coordinated the transportation of food to the affected areas. The distribution was supervised by Clara Barton's associate, Dr. Julian Hubbell, who made a trip to Europe specifically for this task. Even Russians unaffected by the famine were grateful for the American aid. The famous novelist Leo Tolstoy, author of *War and Peace*, specifically singled out Miss Barton for his appreciation.

The Red Cross also stepped in when it received news of suffering in Armenia, then a part of the Ottoman Empire. Armenia was rebelling against repressive Ottoman rule, and thousands of people had been

OTTOMAN EMPIRE

The Ottoman Empire was an empire centered in what is today known as Turkey that existed from 1299 to 1923.

Le Petit Journal

MASSACRES DE CHRETIENS EN TURQUIE

It was well known that the Armenian population suffered greatly under Ottoman rule as it struggled for independence.

killed for helping the resistance efforts. The remaining Armenians had seen their farms damaged and their livelihoods threatened. Various countries offered to send aid and workers, but they were denied the necessary permission. The Ottoman leaders were wary of letting anyone into the country who might support its enemies.

Clara Barton led an international delegation to the Ottoman capital of Constantinople in Turkey, where she hoped to get permission to proceed into the interior. She made it clear that the Red Cross would not pass political judgment on any actions the Ottomans had taken. The Red Cross only wished to provide support to suffering people. When granted permission, Clara stayed in Constantinople to oversee business while others went out into the field. After about six months, the American delegation returned to the United States.

In addition to her many travels, Clara had moved several times during her adult life. Now, in 1897, she built what was to become her final residence in Glen Echo, Maryland. It would also serve as the national headquarters of the American Red

Cross. The large house was a blend of architectural styles. It might not have pleased everyone, but it suited her needs. The house was plain, as she wished, and somewhat resembled a boat. In fact, Clara often referred to her front porch as the main deck. The building also included warehouse facilities where emergency supplies were kept in large quantities.

However, Clara didn't get to enjoy her new home in Glen Echo for very long. Humanitarian problems had surfaced in Cuba. Native Cubans were trying to liberate themselves from the rule of Spain, and the Spanish military forces had dealt with them harshly. Officially, the United States declared itself neutral in the matter. Unofficially, however, Washington favored a free Cuba because it would be more susceptible to American influence. The island had valuable

Clara's large and inviting house in Glen Echo, Maryland, was a combination of home and headquarters.

Clara Barton had an easier time getting volunteers to Cuba than getting her supplies there afterward.

natural resources such as sugar that American business was eager to control.

Whatever the politics of the moment, the Red Cross knew that much of the Cuban population was living in oppressive conditions. Clara Barton was now 75 years old, and she was not feeling particularly well. Still, she intervened with President William McKinley. With his permission, she led a mission to Cuba in January 1898. Her goal was to distribute food and medicine to those in need.

Unfortunately, that need increased a few months later when war was declared between Spain and the United States. The Spanish-American War hampered the Red Cross efforts because the American Navy would not let humanitarian supplies through the naval blockade until its own military forces had landed. This was frustrating, but the Navy rightly feared that any supplies that passed through would end up with the army rather than with suffering people.

Among the arriving troops was a spirited band of volunteers called the Rough Riders. One of their leaders, Lieutenant Colonel Theodore Roosevelt (who would later become President of the United States) met Clara and tried to buy some food for his men. He was told that Red Cross supplies were not for sale. Then how could he acquire some, Roosevelt wanted to know. Just ask, was the reply.

Conditions in the medical camps were horrendous, partly due to the intense heat. "The sight that met us on going into the so-called hospital grounds was something indescribable," Clara later wrote. Soldiers who had been treated had "been compelled to leave all their clothing they had, as too wet, muddy, and bloody to be retained . . ."

By the end of the summer, the war was over. That December, President McKinley addressed Congress on the subject. In his remarks, he specifically mentioned the "the timely and useful work of the Red Cross . . . under the able and experienced leadership of the society, Miss Clara Barton, on the fields of battle and in

The Rough Riders

The Rough Riders was a nickname for the 1st U.S. Volunteer Cavalry. Their forces were added to the regular United States Army, whose numbers were still depleted 30 years after the Civil War. The Rough Riders took part in the Spanish-American War in Cuba under the command of Theodore Roosevelt. He was elected vice president of the United States in 1900 and became president following the assassination of President McKinley.

The Galveston hurricane is widely considered to be the worst natural disaster in American history.

the hospitals at the front..."

Clara returned home satisfied with what she had accomplished. However, she was also aware that criticism of her organizational methods, particularly her reluctance to relinquish control and authority to others, was growing. Now in her late seventies, she had trouble acknowledging the truth of these criticisms, even when they were presented as constructively as possible.

Still, she could not resist the call to confront another catastrophe. In September 1900, a powerful hurricane slammed into Galveston, Texas. The storm hit the city with 135 mile-per-hour winds, an unexpected development because the projected path of the hurricane had followed a more northerly route. At least 6,000 people were killed immediately and the city itself was virtually flattened. Every aspect of the infrastructure, from roads to telephone lines to almost all buildings, was destroyed.

A New York newspaper offered to sponsor Clara's trip to the site. Despite increasing aches and pains, and the unrest over her authority, she felt it was her duty to go. The sight was grim, even for someone with Clara's experience. A thick smog had settled over the city, fed by piles of burning trash and rotting bodies. The horrid smell never dissipated in the two months Clara and her coworkers remained on the scene.

Under Clara's direction, the Red Cross built shelters, fed the homeless, and oversaw the distribution of donations that arrived from all over the nation. Clara was ill at times, but she hid her condition as much as possible so as to continue her work. Again, when the Red Cross was done, it received many thanks for its efforts. During the crisis, Clara managed to ignore the continued rumblings back in Washington over her leadership. When she returned home, however, she had to face them at last.

These rows of tents served as shelters for the many Galveston residents who had lost their homes.

chapter **11**
Final Years

Clara Barton had always prided herself on her ability to run the American Red Cross as she saw fit. And this confidence had served her well for many years. However, she had also received criticism for her somewhat casual accounting practices. These included her habit of keeping records on stray pieces of paper or the backs of envelopes rather than in formal ledgers. No one doubted Clara's honesty or the fairness with which the Red Cross distributed its resources. Still, there were established ways of accounting for spent funds and expenses, and Clara had never followed them. This had not been a problem in the beginning, but once the Red Cross began administering crises on a larger scale,

Clara Barton enjoyed the attention she received during her visit to Russia in 1902.

her unorthodox methods became more noticeable.

Clara had no background in these procedures and no real interest at this point in her life in learning about them. Her priority was helping people. Clearly, some of her methods were better suited to small informal enterprises, than large complicated ones. However, she was more than a little reluctant

Clara never displayed an interest in jewelry, but she was proud of her medal for her work in Russia.

to admit this. Others, particularly some of those now in power in Congress, were not.

Following her efforts in Galveston, Clara headed another American delegation to the International Conference of the Red Cross. The conference was held in St. Petersburg, Russia, during the spring of 1902. During the proceedings, Clara received a Russian medal in recognition of her work, particularly her efforts in Russia 10 years before.

She might have imagined returning home in triumph, but a different kind of welcome awaited her. Clara found herself embroiled in an evolving controversy. Under an act of Congress passed in 1900, the American Red Cross had been reincorporated, or formally reorganized, so that it had to follow new rules and regulations. This change gave it a much closer relationship to the federal government. And yet, when

Clara continued to champion the causes that mattered to her even as old age began to limit her activities.

the Galveston crisis had erupted, Clara had acted with her usual forthright independence. At such times, she did not believe in going to the trouble of calling meetings and taking votes. She acted decisively— just as she always had.

But some people believed that the Red Cross was too much of a one-woman show. Given the changes enacted by Congress, they believed the situation called for a new approach. It was not simply that Clara had gone to Galveston without consulting the Red Cross Executive Board on how to proceed. Her subsequent records concerning the details of how money had been spent were also woefully inadequate.

Clara disagreed. She really didn't see what all the fuss was about. If she had been younger, perhaps she would have been able to approach the situation with more flexibility. At the same time, she had her own dissatisfaction to share. While she had been in Russia, the Red Cross had mounted a relief effort following an earthquake in the West Indies. In her opinion, that effort had been a disaster of its own, poorly executed and not up to her standards. In response, she had moved to consolidate her power even further. At the next annual meeting of the American Red Cross, she engineered the changing of the organization's bylaws so that she was elected president for life and given even more authority than she had previously possessed.

These changes did not take place without protest. Some members of Congress announced their intention to investigate various charges relating to Clara's recent actions. The charges mostly related to the informal way funds were tracked and distributed, but Clara didn't care. She was outraged. In emergencies, there wasn't always time to keep careful records. Desk-bound bureaucrats who never left their offices wouldn't understand that. The investigation later decided the same thing, though it was suggested that if Clara delegated more authority, there would be more people to keep up with the necessary paperwork.

That may have been true, but at 81 years old, Clara was in no mood to change her habits. So in May 1904, she decided to resign. The situation was not ideal, but the time had clearly come. She had always been sensitive to criticism,

THE ..
RED ..
CROSS

Some Facts Concerning
Clara Barton's Work

By WALTER P. PHILLIPS

BRIDGEPORT, CONN.
1903

Before her resignation, books appeared that documented the many accomplishments of Clara's Red Cross years.

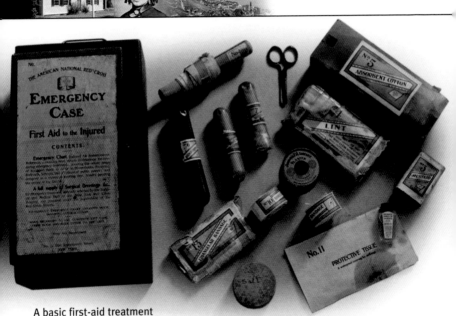

A basic first-aid treatment kit could be used for minor medical needs when a doctor or nurse wasn't available.

and even though no one had accused her of wrongdoing, she disliked having her methods questioned. And so her exit from the organization that she had built from the bottom up was more bitter than she could have ever envisioned.

There were still many issues to sort out, because Clara's personal possessions and property were much entwined with those of the Red Cross. When the two had been essentially the same, no issues had arisen. But now that a formal separation was taking place, there were a lot of legal technicalities to resolve. Fortunately for Clara, it was quickly determined that she would not have to move from the house she had built in Glen Echo, Maryland, even though it also served as the American Red Cross headquarters.

However, retiring from the Red Cross did not mean Clara was ready to spend her time in a rocking chair. That was not her way. Instead, she started another organization, the National First Aid Association of America. Its purpose was to educate the population about proper first-aid treatment, and to ensure the widespread dispersal of first-aid kits.

Putting aside her aches and pains, Clara even did some traveling to promote the National First Aid Association. She once was asked how she managed to endure railway travel, which was assumed to be very tiring, especially for an older person. Her reply reflected much of the practical outlook she had on life. Since she had no control over what happened on board the train, there was no point in worrying about it. She simply put her faith in the conductor and engineer to get the train where it was going without incident. As for passing the time, this was not a

The National First Aid Association of America

When Clara Barton founded the National First Aid Association of America, her goal was to raise public awareness about the importance of first-aid kits and to encourage people to keep them in their homes. Although she lent her energy and name to the organization, she was not involved in its day-to-day operations. The association was later absorbed into the American Red Cross.

Clara's childhood memoir described a place quite different from the modern world she inhabited in the 20th century.

problem. She made notes if she thought of something to write about—and didn't make notes if she didn't. She always brought a book along in case she felt like reading. And if reading made her tired, then she stopped and took a nap. Meanwhile, the train kept rolling along.

Even at her advanced age, Clara stayed busy. She began writing a book called *The Story of My Childhood*. It was to be a definitive account of her early life, but she never entirely finished it. Meanwhile, her daily routine remained firmly established. As her cousin William E. Barton reported in his biography of her life: "She was up with the sun and often before, weeding her garden, feeding her chickens, caring for her pets, and looking after her house." Clara herself confirmed this account of her activities. On February 11, 1910, she wrote in her diary of doing household chores: "At night I fold the wash of Monday for ironing tomorrow. Up at six: commenced ironing and continued till all was done . . ." In the last year of her life, though, she gradually weakened.

There was no sudden medical crisis, but the change was noticeable. On Christmas Day 1911, her 90th birthday, she released a cheerful press notice announcing her intention to enjoy the holiday.

In the spring of 1912, she came down with double pneumonia. The doctors were not hopeful she would ever recover. On April 10, as she lay in bed, she opened her eyes and spoke: "I saw death as it is on the battlefield . . . I saw the surgeons coming, too much needed by all to give special treatment to any one. Once again I stood by them and witnessed those soldiers bearing their soldier pains, limbs being sawed off without opiates being taken, or even a bed to lie on. I crept around once more, trying to give them at least a drink of water to cool their parched lips, and I heard them at last speak of mothers and wives and sweethearts, but never a murmur or complaint."

Two days later, Clara Barton died. She was buried in the Barton family plot near her childhood home in Oxford, Massachusetts. More than 3,000 newspapers took note of her passing. Many tributes were paid to her, including this telling one from the *Detroit Free Press*: "She was perhaps the most perfect incarnation of mercy the modern world has known."

"She was perhaps the most perfect incarnation of mercy the modern world has known."

—The *Detroit Free Press*

chapter **12**

Legacy

The world Clara Barton had entered in 1821 was a very different place from the one she left in 1912. The electric light, the telephone, cars, trains, and airplanes had all made their first appearance during her life. In that time, the population of the United States had grown from just under 10 million to almost a 100 million. At Clara's birth, more than 90 percent of Americans lived in rural areas. By her death, the split between urban and rural was close to even.

These were all significant advances, but just as important was the emerging change in attitude about how people should care for one another. Throughout history, there had always been an urge for one neighbor to help another, to rebuild a barn burned in a fire or to help harvest crops before a bad storm broke. Friends and family often stepped in to nurse others through an illness, and were available for support when times got tough.

But in these instances, the people involved all knew one another. It was

In 1948, the United States Postal Service honored Clara with a stamp for founding the American Red Cross.

different if people received news of a distant catastrophe. They might feel a momentary twinge of sympathy for those affected, but that would soon pass. As for the aftermath of battles and wars, the victors traditionally showed no mercy. The vanquished were killed or taken as slaves, their lands pillaged. Everything of value was either stolen or destroyed. Stories are told that in ancient times, the losers' fields were even sown with salt, an act that would keep the fields barren for generations.

Against this background, the idea of humanitarian aid, help given for its own sake with no payback in mind, was a very modern concept. And its rise in the 19th century was unprecedented. It was given momentum by the International Red Cross, beginning with the Franco-Prussian War in 1871. This example, which Clara Barton witnessed on her visit to Europe, reflected the same attitude and values she had promoted during the Civil War 10 years earlier. The new Red Cross set standards for mercy and humane intervention where none had previously existed.

This tradition continued after Clara's death. By the time World War I ended in 1918, the number of local Red Cross chapters had jumped into the thousands and adult membership had reached 20 million.

In America, the Red Cross was now a cherished institution, one that battled disease and catastrophes wherever they arose. In World War II, the Red Cross was instrumental in caring for military and civilian war victims

Doctors Without Borders currently works in more than 60 countries to improve medical care.

as well as in ferrying 300,000 tons of supplies to soldiers overseas. It also began a national blood program that collected more than 13 million pints of blood for the needs of wounded service personnel. Since then, the organization has continued its mission, fostering medical research and establishing blood banks across the country. Today, although it remains independent of direct government control, the Red Cross works closely with agencies such as the Federal Emergency Management Agency (FEMA) to officially respond to emergencies.

It is also fair to credit the International Red Cross as an inspiration to other organizations that have sprung up over the years. Save the Children, for example, was founded in the United Kingdom in 1919 to improve the educational, economic, and medical conditions of children in disadvantaged areas worldwide. Oxfam was founded in 1942 to combat injustice and poverty across international lines. The charity CARE, which began in 1945, was originally called "Cooperative for American Remittances to Europe," an outgrowth of the American effort to rebuild a world damaged by war.

Today, the organization sponsors projects in more than 60 countries, and is officially known as "Cooperative for Assistance and Relief Everywhere." Doctors Without Borders (Médecins Sans Frontières) was created by doctors and journalists in France in 1971. It is dedicated to bringing medical care to victims of war and disaster. Habitat for Humanity, founded in 1976, is committed to the idea that everyone deserves "a decent, safe, and affordable place to live." The Red Cross, which had pioneered the building of shelters for displaced persons almost 100 years earlier, must have been pleased.

Most significantly, the idea of treating vanquished enemies like human beings, and by extension trying to eliminate the

Save the Children encourages donors to take an ongoing interest in the lives of the children they sponsor.

United Nations

The United Nations is an international organization dedicated to maintaining peace in the world and improving the living conditions of people in need. Its international headquarters is in New York City, with other offices around the world. Originally created with 46 member countries, the U.N. has grown to include 192 member countries, representing the six settled continents of the world.

causes of war underscored the creation of the United Nations. Founded in 1945, after the end of World War II, its primary goal was to keep another world war from ever starting. To do that, it created a platform for countries to discuss their differences and perhaps resolve them without resorting to armed conflict. Concurrently, the U.N. has tackled a wide range of global environmental and social problems. Its human rights and peacekeeping efforts, its educational and medical initiatives, combine to selflessly help regions of the world that are overwhelmed by internal challenges. Its charter states that its goals are to "achieve international co-operation in solving international problems of an economic, social, cultural, or humanitarian character, and in promoting and encouraging respect

CHARTER

A charter is a governing document of an organization that describes its goals.

> *"The United Nations . . . is founded on the principle of the equal worth of every human being."*
>
> —Kofi Annan, in his 2001 speech

for human rights and for fundamental freedoms for all without distinction as to race, sex, language, or religion." And as the seventh secretary-general of the United Nations, Kofi Annan, said in his 2001 Nobel Peace Prize speech, "The United Nations . . . is founded on the principle of the equal worth of every human being."

Clara Barton would be delighted at this sentiment. She was devoted to the idea of helping those in need, regardless of their background or affiliations. The fact that her handiwork contributed to the enduring mission of the Red Cross and inspired other organizations that share her philosophy is a legacy that would make her proud.

Clara's humanitarian work created a helpful example that others have followed, to the world's lasting benefit.

Events in the Life of Clara Barton

1852
Moves to Bordentown, New Jersey to teach school. Successfully establishes a new free school.

December 25, 1821
Clara Barton is born in Oxford, Massachusetts, to Stephen and Sarah Barton.

1860
Returns to Washington, D.C., and resumes working in the Patent Office.

1832–1834
Nurses her seriously injured brother David.

1857
Leaves Washington and returns home to Oxford, Massachusetts.

1867–1868
Travels the country lecturing about her war-time experiences.

1861
Begins volunteering to help soldiers wounded in Civil War.

1863–1865
Travels to help wounded soldiers during various battles.

1854
Becomes a clerk in the U.S. Patent Office in Washington, D.C.

1839
Becomes a teacher in Oxford and nearby communities.

1850
Continues her education at the Clinton Liberal Institute in Clinton, New York.

1865–1867
Supervises attempts to identify Union soldiers missing in action.

1869
Travels to Europe to recover her health. Meets officials of the newly created International Red Cross.

1900
Participates in final relief campaign following a major hurricane in Galveston, Texas.

1881–1895
Participates in a number of Red Cross relief efforts, notably the Johnstown flood in Pennsylvania.

1870–1871
Joins in relief efforts during the Franco-Prussian War.

1902
Leads American participants to International Red Cross conference in Russia.

1877
Begins her efforts to establish the American Red Cross, a process that will take four years.

1896
Leads relief effort to Armenia following oppression by the Ottoman Empire.

1904
Retires from the Red Cross. Initiates the National First Aid Foundation.

April 12, 1912
Dies in Glen Echo, Maryland.

1898
Leads relief effort to Cuba both before and during the Spanish-American War.

1873–1877
Returns home ill and convalesces for the next four years. Moves to Dansville, New York to complete her recovery.

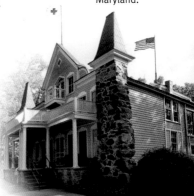

For Further Study

Written by Clara herself, *The Red Cross in Peace and War* (Washington, D.C.: American Historical Press, 1910) tells the story of the American Red Cross.

In *The Life of Clara Barton, Volumes I and II* (Boston: Houghton Mifflin, 1922), William E. Barton gives a detailed account of his famous cousin's life.

Visit the Clara Barton Birthplace Museum in Oxford, Massachusetts to learn more about Clara's life and accomplishments. You can also vistit the online home of the museum at: clarabartonbirthplace.org/sit/?q=node/13

This website summarizes the life of Clara Barton and gives historical information on other people and activities relating to the early years of the Red Cross: www.redcross.org/museum/history/claraBarton.asp

Works Cited

p. 14: "I listened breathlessly . . ." *Illustrious Americans: Clara Barton*, p. 132.

pp.14-15: "I had no playmates . . ." *The Life of Clara Barton, Vol. I*, p. 22.

p. 15: "cling fast to the mane . . ." *Illustrious Americans: Clara Barton*, p. 131.

p. 16: "I was what . . ." *The Life of Clara Barton, Vol. I*, p. 27.

p. 17: "From never having . . ." *Illustrious Americans: Clara Barton*, p. 133.

p. 18: "at length we reached . . ." *Clara Barton Professional Angel*, p. 15.

p. 23: "How well I remember . . ." *Illustrious Americans: Clara Barton*, p. 136.

p. 24: "On entering, I found my little school . . ." ibid.

p. 27: "I may sometimes . . ." *Clara Barton Professional Angel*, p. 15.

p. 29: "in which I should have been . . ." *The Life of Clara Barton, Vol. I*, p. 59.

p. 37: "My situation is delightfully pleasant . . ." *Clara Barton Professional Angel*, p. 57.

p. 38: "obvious impropriety . . ." *Clara Barton Professional Angel*, p. 59.

p. 38: "3,500 pages . . ." *Illustrious Americans: Clara Barton*, p. 144.

p. 40: "It was an oration . . ." Epler, *The Life of Clara Barton*, p. 27.

p. 45: "Nothing is or has been . . ." *Clara Barton Professional Angel*, p. 74.

pp. 45-46: "I have no purpose . . ." *The Portable Abraham Lincoln*, p. 147.

p. 47: "I think the city will be attacked . . ." *Illustrious Americans: Clara Barton*, p. 147.

p. 48: "nothing but their heavy . . ." *The Life of Clara Barton, Vol. I*, p. 109.

pp. 48-49: "Our armies cannot afford . . ." *Illustrious Americans: Clara Barton*, p. 151.

p. 51: "I struggled long and hard . . ." ibid. p. 153.

pp. 51-52: "Go, if it is your duty . . ." Epler, *The Life of Clara Barton*, p. 34.

p. 52: "So far as our poor efforts . . ." *Clara Barton Professional Angel*, p. 79.

p. 53: "five days and nights . . ." *The Life of Clara Barton, Vol. I*, p. 173.

p. 53: "two water buckets . . ." ibid. p. 177.

p. 57: "thanks to our soldiers . . ." *Abraham Lincoln: His Speeches and Writings*, p. 656

p. 59: "from the lion-hearted . . ." Epler, *The Life of Clara Barton*, p. 69.

p. 59: "in the very jaws . . ." ibid.

p. 60: "Think of trying . . ." *The Life of Clara Barton, Vol. I*, p. 219.

p. 61: "the best-protected . . ." *Illustrious Americans: Clara Barton*, p. 172.

p. 61: "shoeless, gloveless . . ." *The Life of Clara Barton, Vol. I*, p. 222.

p. 61: "desolation and pity . . ." ibid.

p. 63: "'Honor any request . . ." *Illustrious Americans: Clara Barton*, p. 40.

p. 63: "I stopped beside . . ." *The Life of Clara Barton, Vol. I*, p. 284.

p. 64: "With malice toward none . . ." *The Portable Abraham Lincoln*, p. 349.

p. 65: "To the Friends . . ." *Clara Barton Professional Angel*, p. 134.

pp. 66-67: "I have looked over . . ." Epler, *The Life of Clara Barton*, p. 117

p. 69: "neither slavery . . ." archives.gov/.../constitution_amendments_11-27.html

p. 69: "right of citizens . . ." ibid.

p. 72: "women don't know . . ." Epler, *The Life of Clara Barton*, p. 397.

p. 72: "I wish men . . ." ibid.

p. 73: "Miss Barton does not . . ." *Clara Barton Professional Angel*, p. 151.

p. 74: "does worse than . . ." ibid. p. 152.

p. 74: "the right to her own property . . ." ibid.

p. 75: "gradually to my horror . . ." *The Life of Clara Barton, Vol. I,* p. 5.

p. 75: "years of unsheltered days. . ." Epler, T*he Life of Clara Barton,* p. 122.

p. 75: "You can't rest . . ." *Illustrious Americans: Clara Barton,* p. 192.

p. 77: "sixteen thousand French . . ." *The Red Cross,* p. 23.

p. 77: "he strongly advocated . . ." ibid.

p. 77-78: "Would it not . . ." *The Life of Clara Barton, Vol. II,* p. 117

p. 79: "with one great . . ." *Illustrious Americans: Clara Barton,* p. 193.

pp. 79-80: " to steer clear . . ." *The World's Great Speeches,* p. 257.

pp. 80-81: "I began to fear . . ." *Angel of the Battlefield: The Life of Clara Barton,* p. 106.

pp. 82-83: "4,000 dead . . ." *Illustrious Americans: Clara Barton,* p. 194.

p. 83: "I saw the work . . . " *The Red Cross in Peace and War,* p. 62.

p. 84: "This population must . . ." *Angel of the Battlefield: The Life of Clara Barton,* p. 115.

pp. 86-87: "Only a small portion . . ." *Illustrious Americans: Clara Barton,* p. 54.

p. 87: "I have in these . . ." ibid. p. 201.

p. 88: "I have done . . ." *The Life of Clara Barton, Vol. I,* p. 96.

p. 88: "I was never . . ." *Illustrious Americans: Clara Barton,* p. 201.

p. 89: "awaken the attention . . ." *The Life of Clara Barton, Vol. I,* p. 126

p. 90: "a treaty under which . . ." *The Life of Clara Barton, Vol. II,* p. 142.

p. 91: "Organized in every State . . ." ibid.

p. 93: "Miss Barton . . ." *The Life of Clara Barton, Vol. I,* p. 150.

p. 93: "the Monroe Doctrine . . ." ibid.

pp. 94-95: "Our skies grew . . ." *The Red Cross in Peace and War,* p. 108.

p. 95: "felt the help and strength . . ." ibid.

p. 95: "energy and perseverance." *Illustrious Americans: Clara Barton,* p. 61.

p. 95: "Our adhesion . . ." *The Life of Clara Barton, Vol. I,* p. 7.

p. 95: "not only in full . . ." Epler, *The Life of Clara Barton,* p. 233.

p. 97: "The day is not far . . ." *The Red Cross in Peace and War,* p. 119.

p. 100: "The wading in mud . . ." *The Red Cross,* p. 157.

p. 105: "The sight that . . ." *The Red Cross in Peace and War,* p. 564.

p. 105: "been compelled to leave . . ." ibid.

p. 105: "the timely and useful . . ." *The Life of Clara Barton, Vol. I,* p. 293.

p. 114: "She was up . . ." *The Life of Clara Barton, Vol. II,* p. 312.

p. 114: "At night I fold . . ." *Illustrious Americans: Clara Barton,* p. 88.

p. 115: "I saw death . . ." Epler, *The Life of Clara Barton,* p. 433.

p. 115: "She was perhaps . . ." ibid, 411.

p. 119: "a decent, . . ." habitat.org/how/default.aspx

p. 120-121: "achieve international co-operation . . ." *Encyclopedia of Human Rights Issues Since 1945,* p. 291.

p. 121: "The United Nations . . ." nobelprize.org/nobel_prizes/peace/laureates/2001/annan-lecture.html

Bibliography

Barton, Clara. *The Red Cross, a history of this remarkable international movement in the interest of humanity.* Washington, D. C., American national Red Cross, 1898.

Barton, Clara. *The Red Cross in Peace and War.* Washington, D.C.: American Historical Press, 1910

Barton, William E. *The Life of Clara Barton, Volumes I and II* Boston: Houghton Mifflin, 1922.

Basler, Roy P., ed. *Abraham Lincoln: His Speeches and Writings.* Cleveland: World Pub. Co., 1956,

Copeland Lewis et al, eds. *The World's Great Speeches.* Mineola, NY: Dover Publications, 1999,

Delbanco, Andrew, ed. *The Portable Abraham Lincoln.* New York: Penguin Books, 2009.

Epler, Percy H. *The Life of Clara Barton.* New York: The Macmillan Company, 1917.

Fishwick, Marshall W. *Illustrious Americans: Clara Barton.* Morristown, NJ: Silver Burdett Company, 1966.

Langley, Winston E. *Encyclopedia of Human Rights Issues Since 1945.* Westport, CT: Greenwood Press, 1999.

Pryor, Elizabeth Brown. *Clara Baron Professional Angel.* Philadelphia: University of Pennsylvania Press, 1987.

Ross, Ishbel. *Angel of the Battlefield: The Life of Clara Barton.* New York: Harper & Brothers, 1956.

Williams, Blanche Colton. *Clara Barton: Daughter of Destiny.* Philadelphia: J.P. Lippincott, 1941.

Index

Author's acknowledgments

My thanks to Shannon Beatty for her editorial comments and encouragement while keeping me on schedule, to Emily Thomas of the Clara Barton Birthplace Museum for her valuable input, and to my wife Joan for always being such a reliable a sounding board.

Picture Credits

Front Cover Photo: Library of Congress

Back Cover Photo: The Barton Center for Diabetes Education, Inc.

The photographs in this book are used with permission and through the courtesy of (t=top; b=bottom; l=left; r=right; c=center; a=above):

SuperStock: pp.1, 79TL, 123TCB; The Barton Center for Diabetes Education, Inc.: pp.6, 116, 122TL; Architect of the Capitol: p.8; Library of Congress: pp.9, 13, 14, 15, 17, 19, 25, 26, 28, 29, 32, 33, 34, 36, 37, 39, 41, 42, 43, 45, 48, 51B, 52, 53, 55, 57T, 58, 59, 60T, 61, 62, 63, 64, 66, 67, 68, 70, 71, 75B, 76, 77, 85, 88, 89, 91, 92, 93, 94, 95, 100, 101, 104, 105, 106, 107, 110, 122TC/TR/BC, 123TL/TC/BL; Bridgeman Art Library; p.11 National Gallery of Scotland; p.18 Bridgeman Art Library; p.20 AISA; p.44 Peter Newark Military Pictures; p.83 Pushkin Museum; Clara Barton National Historic Site or Glen Echo Park: pp.12, 24, 51T, 65, 99, 103, 109, 111, 112, 114, 121, 122BL/BR, 123TR/BR; Getty Images: pp.16, 47, 50, 96, 118, 119; 120 Karl Shone; p.75T Time&Life Pictures; North Wind Picture Archives: pp. 21, 30, 80; Alamy Images: pp.22, 98; pp.11, 54 frame Mark Sykes Picture Frames; The Print Collector: p.35 North Wind Picture Archives; p.69 The Art Archive; p.72 Mary Evans Picture Library; p.79B, 81, 84 Interfoto; The Granger Collection: pp.23, 73, 108; Corbis: pp.31, 40, 60B, 82 Bettman; pp.56, 57B William A. Bake; p.90 C.I.C.R./Sygma/ Vernier Jean Bern; National Park Service: pp.46, 54; National Museum of Civil War Medicine: p.49; DK Images: p.79T, 87; The Image Works: p.102 Roger Violett; Scripophily.com: p.113. **Border Images**, left to right: Barton Center for Diabetes Education, Inc., Clara Barton National Historic Site or Glen Echo Park, Library of Congress, Library of Congress, Library of Congress, Clara Barton National Historic Site or Glen Echo Park

Other DK Biographies you'll enjoy:

Abigail Adams
Kem Knapp Sawyer
ISBN 978-0-7566-5209-8 paperback
ISBN 978-0-7566-5208-1 hardcover

Marie Curie
Vicki Cobb
ISBN 978-0-7566-3831-3 paperback
ISBN 978-0-7566-3832-0 hardcover

Charles Darwin
David C. King
ISBN 978-0-7566-2554-2 paperback
ISBN 978-0-7566-2555-9 hardcover

Princess Diana
Joanne Mattern
ISBN 978-0-7566-1614-4 paperback
ISBN 978-0-7566-1613-7 hardcover

Amelia Earhart
Tanya Lee Stone
ISBN 978-0-7566-2552-8 paperback
ISBN 978-0-7566-2553-5 hardcover

Thomas Edison
Jan Adkins
ISBN 978-0-7566-5207-4 paperback
ISBN 978-0-7566-5206-7 hardcover

Albert Einstein
Frieda Wishinsky
ISBN 978-0-7566-1247-4 paperback
ISBN 978-0-7566-1248-1 hardcover

Benjamin Franklin
Stephen Krensky
ISBN 978-0-7566-3528-2 paperback
ISBN 978-0-7566-3529-9 hardcover

Gandhi
Amy Pastan
ISBN 978-0-7566-2111-7 paperback
ISBN 978-0-7566-2112-4 hardcover

Harry Houdini
Vicki Cobb
ISBN 978-0-7566-1245-0 paperback
ISBN 978-0-7566-1246-7 hardcover

Thomas Jefferson
Jacqueline Ching
ISBN 978-0-7566-4506-9 paperback
ISBN 978-0-7566-4505-2 hardcover

Helen Keller
Leslie Garrett
ISBN 978-0-7566-0339-7 paperback
ISBN 978-0-7566-0488-2 hardcover

Joan of Arc
Kathleen Kudlinksi
ISBN 978-0-7566-3526-8 paperback
ISBN 978-0-7566-3527-5 hardcover

John F. Kennedy
Howard S. Kaplan
ISBN 978-0-7566-0340-3 paperback
ISBN 978-0-7566-0489-9 hardcover

Martin Luther King, Jr.
Amy Pastan
ISBN 978-0-7566-0342-7 paperback
ISBN 978-0-7566-0491-2 hardcover

Abraham Lincoln
Tanya Lee Stone
ISBN 978-0-7566-0834-7 paperback
ISBN 978-0-7566-0833-0 hardcover

Nelson Mandela
Lenny Hort & Laaren Brown
ISBN 978-0-7566-2109-4 paperback
ISBN 978-0-7566-2110-0 hardcover

Mother Teresa
Maya Gold
ISBN 978-0-7566-3880-1 paperback
ISBN 978-0-7566-3881-8 hardcover

Annie Oakley
Chuck Wills
ISBN 978-0-7566-2997-7 paperback
ISBN 978-0-7566-2986-1 hardcover

Barack Obama
Stephen Krensky
ISBN 978-0-7566-5805-2 paperback
ISBN 978-0-7566-5804-5 hardcover

Ronald Reagan
Michael Burgan
ISBN 978-0-7566-7074-0 paperback
ISBN 978-0-7566-7075-7 hardcover

Eleanor Roosevelt
Kem Knapp Sawyer
ISBN 978-0-7566-1496-6 paperback
ISBN 978-0-7566-1495-9 hardcover

Harriet Tubman
Kem Knapp Sawyer
ISBN 978-0-7566-5806-9 paperback
ISBN 978-0-7566-5807-6 hardcover

George Washington
Lenny Hort
ISBN 978-0-7566-0835-4 paperback
ISBN 978-0-7566-0832-3 hardcover

Laura Ingalls Wilder
Tanya Lee Stone
ISBN 978-0-7566-4508-3 paperback
ISBN 978-0-7566-4507-6 hardcover